Other books: Harold W. Stevenson

Iscoe, I., and Stevenson, H.W., eds. (1960). *Personality Development in Children*. Austin: University of Texas Press.

Stevenson, H.W., ed. (1963). *62nd Yearbook of the National Society for the Study of Education, Child Psychology*. Chicago: University of Chicago Press.

Stevenson, H.W., Hess, E.H., and Rheingold, H.L., eds. (1967). *Early Behavior: Comparative and Developmental Approaches*. New York: Wiley.

Stevenson, H.W. (1972). *Children's Learning*. New York: Appleton-Century Crofts. Japanese translation by A. Sadao, Y. Kobayashi, & O. Shigetoshi. Tokyo: Taiken Shuppan Kabushikikaisha, 1981.

Stevenson, H.W., co-ed. (1978). *Psychology: From Research to Practice*. New York: Plenum.

Wagner, D., and Stevenson, H.W., eds. (1981). *Cross-cultural Studies of Child Development*. San Francisco: Freeman.

Paris, S., Olson, G.M., and Stevenson, H.W., eds. (1982). *Learning and Motivation in the Classroom*. Hillsdale, NJ: Erlbaum.

Stevenson, H.W., and Jing, C.C., eds. (1984). *Conference Proceedings: Issues in Cognition*. Washington, DC: American Psychological Association.

Stevenson, H.W., and Siegel, A.E., eds. (1984). *Research in Child Development and Social Policy*. Chicago: University of Chicago Press.

Stevenson, H.W., Asuma, H., and Hakuta, K., eds. (1986). *Child Development and Education in Japan*. New York: Freeman.

Other books: James W. Stigler

Stigler, J. W., Shweder, R. A., and Herdt, G., eds. (1990). *Cultural Psychology: Essays in Comparative Human Development*. New York: Cambridge University Press.

Stigler, J. W., Lee, S. Y., and Stevenson, H. W. (1990). *Mathematical Knowledge of Japanese, Chinese, and American Elementary School Children*. Reston, VA: National Council of Teachers of Mathematics.

The Learning Gap

Why Our Schools Are Failing and What We Can Learn from Japanese and Chinese Education

Harold W. Stevenson
and James W. Stigler

A TOUCHSTONE BOOK
Published by Simon & Schuster
New York London Toronto Sydney Tokyo Singapore

TOUCHSTONE
Rockefeller Center
1230 Avenue of the Americas
New York, New York 10020

First Touchstone Edition 1994
TOUCHSTONE and colophon are registered trademarks of
Simon & Schuster Inc.
Designed by Irving Perkins Associates
Manufactured in the United States of America

20 19 18 17 16 15 14 13 12 11

Library of Congress Cataloging-in-Publication Data
Stevenson, Harold W. (Harold William)
  The learning gap : why our schools are failing and what we
can learn from Japanese and Chinese education / Harold W.
Stevenson, James W. Stigler.
    p.   cm.
  Includes bibliographical references and index.
  1. Education, Elementary—United States.   2. Education,
Elementary—Japan.   3. Education, Elementary—
Taiwan.   4. Comparative education.   I. Stigler, James W.
II. Title.
LA219.S76   1992
372.973—dc20   91-44409
                                                     CIP

ISBN 0-671-70983-6
ISBN 0-671-88076-4 (PBK)

Figure 1.1 by Dick Locher © 1987 by the *Chicago Tribune*.
Reprinted by permission of Tribune Media Services.

Figure 2.1 © 1987 by Bill Plympton. Reprinted by permission.

Contents

Preface

The research on which this book is based started in the mid-1970s, when Americans began to be greatly concerned about the high incidence of reading disabilities found among American children. At that time, claims were made that Chinese and Japanese children did not have such disabilities. If these claims were true, it was suggested, then the explanation of many reading problems might reside in the writing systems used for the different languages. Written English, it was argued, is difficult to read because there is low correspondence between the way words are written and the way they are pronounced. Chinese and Japanese, on the other hand, are more regular in terms of symbol-sound relations, and have the added advantage of using distinctive characters to represent different words.

Stevenson visited China during this time as part of the first delegation of American child development experts to visit that country since 1949. Based on that experience, and also on earlier experience in learning Japanese, he doubted that differences in writing systems alone could explain differences in reading achievement between Chinese, Japanese, and American children. In 1976 he began planning what turned out to be the first in a series of large cross-cultural studies focused on the roots of academic achievement in East Asia and the United States. He traveled to

Taiwan and Japan to find researchers who would be willing to collaborate in a large-scale study. Stigler, who had studied Chinese in college, arrived in Ann Arbor in 1977 to begin working on his Ph.D. and immediately joined the project.

The findings from that first study were surprising in several respects. First, the claim that Japanese and Chinese children did not display reading disabilities proved to be unfounded. When they were tested with culturally fair and appropriate materials, the percentage of children in Taiwan and Japan who evidenced severe problems in learning to read was not found to differ from the percentage in the United States. What did differ, however, were the ways that parents, teachers, and children thought about "disabilities" in these different cultures. Americans, it turned out, were more willing than were Japanese and Chinese to attribute children's academic successes and failures to innate abilities and disabilities; the Asians referred more to environmental factors and children's own effort in their explanations of school performance. These different beliefs, and the implications they have for the design of educational systems in the different cultures, are part of the story we tell in this book.

Even more surprising were the results from tests of mathematics that we included in the study in order to evaluate the generality of children's learning problems. Although the American children did not fare especially badly in reading, their scores in mathematics were markedly below those of their Asian peers. Why this should be the case is a question that we have tried to answer in the studies we have summarized in this book.

We want to mention several things about the stylistic approach we have adopted. We have written this book so that it can be understood by the nonspecialist. As a result, we have omitted all reference to statistical analyses. We should point out, however, that whenever we state that relationships between variables are significant, or that the value of one variable is greater than that of another, we mean that statistical tests have revealed that these effects are not due to chance. The reader who is interested in the statistical basis of our comments should read our more technical publications. We have included references to these publications in a list of further reading at the back of the book.

Throughout the book we have used the term Asian as a shorthand reference to Chinese and Japanese societies. We realize that the more accurate term is East Asian, and that there is more to East Asia than Taiwan, China, and Japan. Similarly, we realize that our discussion is based on an intimate knowledge of schools and families in five large metropolitan areas and not on national samples. We chose five cities for our studies because of their representativeness, and expect that similar results would be obtained in other large cities in these countries. Whether or not this expectation is correct is a matter that can be decided only through further research.

The reader should also keep in mind that our discussion concerns elementary schools. All of the research on which this book is based was conducted in elementary schools, and in many respects the elementary schools of China and Japan, as well as the United States, differ markedly from the high schools. More is known about high schools in these cultures than about elementary schools. When our account contradicts the reader's prior impressions, remember that those impressions are probably based on reports of high schools, not elementary schools.

Finally, we want to warn the reader that our writing focuses more often on the positive aspects of Asian education and parenting than on the problems. This makes us appear, at times, overly critical of the American system of education and child-rearing. Of course, there are many problems in the ways Asians rear and educate their children, just as there are virtues and strengths in American practices. Our goal, however, is not to provide a balanced assessment of the strengths and weaknesses of the Asian and American systems. Instead, we want to explore ways in which the United States might improve its educational system by learning from the successes of other cultures.

. . .

Although two of us wrote this book, we could not have done so without the collaboration of a large group of colleagues in China, Japan, Taiwan, and the United States. The book draws heavily on a series of articles and monographs that this group has already published and on additional work that will be published in the near future.

We are especially grateful to Shinying Lee and Chuansheng Chen of the University of Michigan; Ada Hegion and Darlene Stealey of Minneapolis; Seiro Kitamura, Susumu Kimura, and the late Tadahisa Kato of Tohoku Fukushi University in Sendai, Japan; Chen-chin Hsu of the Cheng Gung University Hospital in Tainan and Lian-wen Mao of Taipei Municipal Teachers College in Taiwan; and Fang Ge, Tong Lequan, and the late Liu Fan, of the Institute of Psychology of the Chinese Academy of Sciences in Beijing. Our work depended also on the participation of many others, including Veronica Ichikawa, G. William Lucker, Max Lummis, Michelle Perry, Ailan Tsao, and David Uttal. All of us who have been involved in the research are deeply indebted to the principals, teachers, parents, and children who so kindly agreed to join us in our efforts to understand cultural influences on children's academic achievement.

We wrote most of the book during 1990 while we were Fellows at the Center for Advanced Study in the Behavioral Sciences at Stanford, California. Our stay was made possible by support from the Spencer Foundation, and in the case of Stigler, a Guggenheim Fellowship. We are deeply grateful for the opportunity we had to spend this time at the Center, and want to express our thanks to the director, Philip E. Converse, and the associate director, Robert A. Scott, for inviting us; to Kathleen Much, who helped us a great deal in clarifying our statements of our ideas; and to the other Fellows with whom we had many fruitful discussions. The research on which this book is based was supported by grants to Stevenson from the National Institute of Mental Health, the National Science Foundation, and the William T. Grant Foundation;

and to Stigler from the Spencer Foundation. None of these agencies is responsible, of course, for what we have written.

Many people have helped us by reading and criticizing earlier drafts of this book. We especially want to thank Jean Aptakin, Peter Aptakin, Lisa Baker, Chuansheng Chen, James Hiebert, Shinying Lee, Sheila Sconiers, Laura Skidmore, Alice Smuts, Robert Smuts, Tom Stigler, and Janet Zimmerman. We would also like to thank Katinka Matson for lending her enthusiasm to the project in its early stages and for leading us to our able editor, Robert Asahina.

We are indebted to our wives, Nancy Stevenson and Karen Aptakin Stigler, who have read every chapter with a critical eye and have made many suggestions for improving the manuscript.

Finally, this book was a shared effort from the initial organization and writing to the final editing. Both authors participated fully in its conception and writing, and first authorship could have belonged to either of us. If the book speaks with one voice, it is because of this close interaction, from which we have learned a great deal. We hope that the result is a clear, readable, and useful contribution to the discussion of one of the nation's most pressing problems—the education of its children.

—H. W. S., J. W. S.

Chapter 1

Introduction

It is no secret by now that American education is in crisis. Teachers work long hours for little reward. Our children's academic achievement is in decline. We pour more money into our schools, but we don't see a corresponding improvement in quality. Especially in mathematics and science, American children trail their counterparts in Europe and Asia, and they are losing ground.

The current educational crisis reverberates beyond the classroom, for a poorly educated work force directly hampers a nation's productivity and economic competitiveness. A modern, productive worker must be literate and must know basic mathematics and science. Unfortunately, in the United States fewer and fewer children learn much in our classrooms. American businesses now spend more than $25 billion each year on remedial education for their employees—virtually all of whom are products of the nation's public schools.[1] The lamentably high percentages of our citizens who are illiterate, ignorant of government and geography, and unable to write clear and coherent sentences should cause deep concern in a democracy that relies on an informed population. The very quality of life in a modern nation clearly reflects the educational level of its citizens.

Although articles describing the educational crisis appear almost daily in the nation's press, and although the 1989 summit meeting on education between the President and the nation's governors reflects an awareness of its immense proportions, discussions of the crisis seldom go beyond sober political pronouncements and hastily drawn, simplistic solutions.

It is evident that our schools are failing the American public. The important question this educational crisis raises is, How can we make changes that will reverse this process?

This book rests on the premise that the crisis in American education can be resolved only when all of us—parents, teachers, school administrators, and citizens—step back and examine our basic assumptions about the educational process. We must tackle difficult questions about the motivations, beliefs, attitudes, and practices that underlie the ponderous entity we call American education. This is not an easy assignment, but until we have a better grasp of these complex issues, we are unlikely to move any closer to solutions than we are today.

The two of us do not speak as educators. We are social scientists—psychologists by training—who have spent our professional lives studying children's growth and development. We have the audacity to write about education because we have been studying the development of Chinese, Japanese, and American children for more than a decade, and we see overwhelming differences in some aspects of these cultures that affect the educational process.

Our focus has been on elementary school children and their parents and teachers. We have studied the children's daily environments both in school and out. We have visited hundreds of classrooms, heard from thousands of parents and children, and observed scores of teachers in China, Japan, Taiwan, and the United States. Much of what we have discovered is new, for there were no comparative studies of such magnitude in these cultures before we began our work. With this background of experience

14

and with the scientific data to support our conclusions, we believe that we can improve our readers' understanding of the American educational system and suggest changes that should be made in the system.

THE BIG DEBATE

In the 1980s, Americans debated how to reform American schools. Committees and commissions churned out countless reports, books, and other documents throughout the decade. Often they proposed simple remedies—more money, choice of schools, smaller classes, higher standards, and merit pay—all of which sounded reasonable and stimulated changes in many states. In view of the meager outcomes that these changes have generally yielded, however, we think it is unlikely that any of them, singly or in combination, can produce enough improvement to reverse the process of deterioration in American schools.

Segments of our findings made their way into some of these discussions, but until now we have not had the opportunity to bring our results and conclusions together in a single publication. That is what we seek to do in this book. What we have to offer is a new slant on American life as we contrast what our culture has to say about children and schooling with what we found in China, Japan, and Taiwan.

MAKING THE FAMILIAR STRANGE

Our schools and families exist within the cultural context of American society. Without knowledge about how culture influences educational and child-rearing practices, it is difficult to perceive, let alone respond to, some of our most fundamental national characteristics. Paradoxically, the more widely practices and beliefs are shared within a society, the harder it is to see them.

We become accustomed to the aspects of our environment that we encounter frequently. Sheer familiarity dims the keenness of our perception, and we cease to notice a good deal of what goes on in our daily lives; what we do to teach our children becomes routine. In order to shake ourselves into awareness, we must experience new or contrasting conditions.

Meaning often emerges through contrast. We do not know what it means to work hard until we see how hard others work. We do not understand what children can accomplish until we have seen what other children the same age do. So it is with cultures. Cross-cultural comparisons can help us discover characteristics of our own culture that we fail to notice because we are so familiar with them. Through such comparisons, our perceptions become clearer and sharper. In fact, we are stunned at times to realize that what we have thought to be ordinary is actually very unusual in other cultures.

For example, several years ago we visited a mathematics class in a Japanese elementary school where the children were learning to draw cubes in three dimensions. One boy was having trouble. His cube looked crooked, no matter how carefully he tried to copy the lines from the teacher's model. Seeing the child's difficulties, the teacher asked him to go to the blackboard and draw his cube. After working for five or ten minutes, he asked the teacher to look at his work. Rather than judging the child's efforts herself, she turned to the class and asked whether the drawing was correct. The child's classmates shook their heads no. The teacher directed the boy to try again. He struggled until the end of the forty-minute class. As time passed, we began to feel more and more uncomfortable and anxious about the child at the board. What must he be feeling? Would he burst into tears? Yet he appeared to be undisturbed by his public exposure and gave no indication of crying. By the end of the class he had drawn a passable cube, and the class applauded.

Scenes like this are not unusual in Chinese and Japanese classrooms, and later we will show how this one fits into the broader context of Asian education. For now, we want to focus on how the experience affected us. Because American teachers fear public failure might damage a child's self-esteem, they generally do not send children to the blackboard to display their errors to the whole class. Moreover, Americans conceive of errors as a possible precursor of ultimate failure. People should strive to avoid errors and to give only the correct response—a routine that fits our culture and has been strengthened by the writings of behavioral psychologists such as B. F. Skinner.

Japanese and Chinese teachers and students have a different view. They regard mistakes as an index of what still needs to be learned. They expect that with persistence and effort, people will eliminate errors and eventually make the correct response. In the Japanese classroom, the child struggling at the board was displaying a positive, not a negative characteristic. His errors were not a matter of great concern; what would be worrisome would be the child's failure to expend the effort necessary to correct them. This experience gave us a new appreciation of how errors, rather than being an index of failure, can be put to positive use in learning.

Melford Spiro, the anthropologist, in a phrase borrowed from T. S. Eliot, described good anthropology as that which "makes the familiar strange, and the strange familiar."[2] This phrase summarizes what we hope to accomplish in this book. Having compared teaching, parenting, learning, and academic achievement in several very different cultures, we found the most exciting revelations not in what we discovered in Asia, but in what was revealed in the United States. Despite the fact that we have spent all our lives in this country, we, as is likely true of most Americans, had never really understood the consequences of many American beliefs, attitudes, and practices until we began our studies in Asia. Many aspects of American education began to seem strange when we viewed them through lenses altered by our Asian experience. We have experienced the thrill—and the distress—of discovering new attributes of our culture.

OUR NATIONAL DEFENSIVENESS

If it was ever fashionable to study and learn from Asian cultures, it certainly is not now. Americans feel battered by comparisons with Asians, and with the Japanese in particular. We often feel justifiably defensive about such comparisons. But what are the costs of ignoring the global context in which we live? And what misconceptions of ourselves might we perpetuate by failing to look outward, toward sights that could illuminate our self-perceptions? It is unsettling to realize that Americans, on average, have little real interest in the study of other nations and cultures. As a consequence, our image of others often is cast in stereotypes.

The accompanying cartoon appeared in *The Chicago Tribune*.[3] In the left panel, American observers, peering intently into the Japanese classroom, are recording every detail for presumed later analysis. In the right panel are Japanese investigators, howling with laughter outside the American classroom. The cartoon taps our worst fears.

But does it represent reality? We think not. In the first place, the depiction of Japanese laughing at the American educational system is in our experience entirely wrong. Japanese see weaknesses in our system, but they are not laughing at all. Rather, they view these weaknesses as a serious threat to the economies of both the United States and Japan. The problem, they believe, is to get Americans to take our weakened educational system as seriously as the Japanese do—and to do something about it. That was the message carried by the Japanese delegation to the U.S.–Japan bilateral trade talks in the fall of 1989. They argued that Japan cannot be held solely to blame for the enormous American trade deficit and that at least part of the problem must be traced to America's lack of the educated work force that is required for industrial excellence.

But Asians also see real strengths in the American educational

system, and they are serious about learning from its positive aspects. Three strengths in particular are often mentioned in our conversations with Asian educators and parents.

Wherever one goes in Asia, one hears the complaint that although Chinese and Japanese students show high levels of academic achievement, they lack creativity, a characteristic Asians believe is more prevalent in American students than in their own. Committees appointed by Asian ministries of education are frequently charged with finding ways to foster greater creativity among their students.

A related strength is that Americans seem to avoid the excruciating competition that Asian students appear to face in their quest for places in prestigious universities. The use of scores on entrance examinations as the sole criterion for admission to universities has led Asian high school students to spend inordinate amounts of time on their studies—attending regular classes and after-school cram schools and doing schoolwork at home. The apparently more easygoing American high school students seem to avoid this trauma, and Asian educators have asked whether they should continue their strong reliance on entrance exams.

A third area of perceived strength lies in American universities. The large number of Asian students who seek admission to graduate schools in the United States indicates the high regard in which American higher education is held in Asia. Asians perceive their own universities as weak. Life at even the best universities, especially in Japan, is derided as a time of rest and recreation between the grueling battles that precede and follow the undergraduate years. Attendance at university classes is poor, expectations are low, and students regard the undergraduate years as a four-year vacation from the process of becoming a productive citizen.

But what about the other panel of the cartoon? How serious are Americans about learning from Asian cultures? That depiction is at odds with reality as well. If recent studies are an indication, many Americans can't even locate Asian nations on a world map,[4] and they certainly have little interest in the possible benefits of studying these seemingly remote and exotic foreign cultures.

STEREOTYPES

Taking an interest in Asian education does not mean that we should, or can, adopt the successful aspects of Asian systems of child-rearing and education. They are adaptive for the cultures in which they exist, and our problems are not going to be solved by importing Chinese or Japanese culture. Instead, we must find the resources within our own culture that made America great in the first place. "If we have to out-cooperate and out-sacrifice the Japanese, we may as well quit. We need . . . to find our own tools," suggested James Fallows in his discussion of Japanese and American competitiveness.[5] But if we perpetuate biased, stereotyped views of ourselves as well as of others, we won't accomplish this.

What are our biased views? Here are some examples of common stereotypes that Americans hold about Asians, especially with regard to their educational success:

- Asian children are under great stress from very early ages; they exhibit great tension and even suicidal tendencies because of the demands placed on them by their teachers and parents.
- Asian children are far easier to teach in school than American children because they are innately docile.
- Asian teaching methods stress rote learning, relying on endless, mindless drill of basic skills.
- Asian children do well in school because their parents push them, training them in academic skills beginning in early childhood.

These examples will suffice, although there are many others. As will become clear in the chapters that follow, these stereotypes are largely inaccurate, especially as they pertain to younger children. Americans have false ideas about both the investment required and the costs involved in attaining high levels of academic achievement. More important, these stereotypes allow us to maintain a view of ourselves as relaxed, successful, effective individualists who are creative, innovative, and independent. Such stereotypes at best are inaccurate and at worst undermine efforts to overcome our problems.

The first stereotype—that Asians put enormous pressure on their young children to learn academic skills—is an oft-cited indictment of the costs associated with high levels of academic achievement. As we will show, it is inaccurate. Although pressure builds during the high school years, when concerns about university entrance exams intensify, such pressure is not evident during the preschool or elementary school years, a time when levels of achievement already are high. Asian children work hard, but we know of no evidence that they suffer greater psychological distress or a greater incidence of suicide than exists in Western children.[6] But that is not the point we wish to make here. Embedded in this stereotype of the unacceptable cost of high achievement in Asia is a widely held vision of America: We are a people, it says, who value play in childhood, who let children grow to fulfill their unique potential rather than be fitted into a uniform national mold, and who have greater sources of personal fulfillment than learning a narrow set of academic skills.

But is this view of ourselves accurate? We will argue that our self-view is no more accurate than our view of Asians, and that our ignorance of other cultures is useful for maintaining a lack of self-awareness about our own cultural stance on issues relating to education and child development.

We can go through the other stereotypes listed above and see that each one is colored by some aspect of our self-view. In perceiving Asian children as docile, we impute to our own children the qualities of liveliness and assertiveness. In deriding Asian teaching methods as rote, we define our own methods as flexible and innovative. In suggesting that rote learning is pervasive in Asian classrooms, we exaggerate the levels of creativity that result from the American educational process. And in contending that Asian children are hurried into acquiring academic skills by their parents, we congratulate ourselves on preserving childhood for our children.

In a similar vein, we cite the fact that more Nobel Prizes have gone to Americans than to Chinese or Japanese as proof that we have little to learn from studying how Asians go about educating their children. These false notions about others and about ourselves serve to obscure from view the realities of our own behavior.

SEARCHING FOR SOLUTIONS

President Bush's education summit with the nation's governors issued yet another set of reform-oriented pronouncements,[7] whose primary significance lay in their having been approved unanimously by the participants. The governors offered the nation six goals for improving schools by the year 2000. These goals included having all children entering school "ready to learn," decreasing the dropout rate, increasing adult literacy, and having

American students rank number one in the world in mathematics and science.

Stating goals is laudable, but we are far from achieving any of these. To hear them stated so glibly with no reference to how they would be attained jars us into facing the great gap between goal and accomplishment. Without a vast expansion of early childhood education programs, there is no way all American children can enter school in the year 2000 ready to learn the first-grade curriculum. The dropout rate will remain high as long as students perceive—correctly—that the minimal level of knowledge and skills required for graduation prepares them for little more than low-level service jobs. Reducing adult illiteracy requires programs that capitalize on techniques that appeal to adult students. And if we do not make profound changes in our mathematics and science curricula, the goal of becoming number one in the world in these areas is absurd.

We must gain a better understanding of the causes of our problems before we can even contemplate how to reach the governors' goals. Yet the public discussion that followed the governors' conference moved quickly to the question of who will pay for achieving the goals, without first deciding what would be done if money were available. Money has not solved the problems of education. Improving education may cost more money, but the truth is that educators charged with improving our schools do not know how best to spend our educational reform dollars. They lack the information necessary to make such decisions. The reason is not hard to find: In the United States, little money is spent on educational research—that is, on finding out which educational initiatives work and which do not. In fact, in a report issued in 1987, the U.S. General Accounting Office found that from the early 1970s through the mid-1980s—the period when American educational deficiencies began to be a topic of national concern—the U.S. Department of Education decreased its support for research more than 70 percent in constant dollars. During the same period, federal spending for education in general increased 38 percent.[8] Figuratively, we are buying limousines for transport, without drawing any maps to show us which roads might lead us out of the morass.

School reforms initiated in Chicago and in Minnesota exemplify movements based on beliefs and hopes rather than on solid information. Political forces in Chicago believe local control is the key to school reform, and have restructured the school system by transferring significant power from the board of education to local school councils. Similarly, educational policymakers in Minnesota believe that parents should have the opportunity to choose the schools their children attend. Presumably, like businesses in a market economy, better schools will flourish and inferior schools will either close or improve.

These reforms may in fact lead to improvement in the schools of Chicago and Minnesota. But if they do not, resources and energy will have been wasted on experiments of enormous scale. In our zeal to initiate changes, we run the risk of evoking discouragement that anything can ever be done to solve our problems in education. This is further reason that we might benefit from looking at other countries, to see how they have succeeded—or how they have failed.

IN DEFENSE OF TEACHERS, PARENTS, AND CHILDREN

It might seem from the above that our concern is primarily with the schools, and indeed, ultimately it is. But schools exist in a society composed in part of teachers, parents, and children. It is to these three groups that we will direct most of our attention in this book. Just as it is easy to suggest that children's achievement would be improved if more hours were spent in school, it is equally easy to suggest that all our problems can be traced to the ineptitude of American teachers, parents, and children.

American teachers are especially likely targets of criticism.

They would be more effective, it is charged, if they were better educated. As we will see later, however, their levels of formal education are higher than those of Chinese and Japanese teachers. Another charge is that they come to class improperly prepared for each day's lesson. This criticism is particularly unfair, for as we will see, American teachers are allowed little time for preparation outside the classroom.

Parents, too, are often criticized as the source of children's poor achievement. They are portrayed as being uninterested, unsupportive, and so immersed in their own problems that they have little time to attend to or interact with their children. In some cases they are, but the complaint heard from most parents is that they feel estranged from their children's schools. They don't know what they should be doing or how they should go about doing it. Perhaps as a consequence of the introduction of new approaches to teaching mathematics and science more than twenty years ago, the gulf between home and school has widened. As we will see, American parents begin to abdicate responsibility for their children's education soon after the children enter first grade, and they place ever increasing demands on the school. The situation is probably the fault of neither the present-day schools nor the parents. Yet, at the same time, schools clearly cannot handle the job of education without the involvement, support, and encouragement of parents.

American children, it is claimed, are inattentive and unwilling to work hard in school, and they demand a fast-paced daily life and an easy resolution of problems that parallel what they see in the television programs that occupy so much of their time. Indeed, many people maintain that the inordinate amount of time American children spend in front of the television set is a serious impediment to their education. From our data, however, we will see that Japanese children spend even more time watching television— while greatly surpassing American children in their academic performance. The influence of television may not always be positive, but in itself it is not the menace that it is often painted to be.

Why might children be inattentive in school? One likely reason is that they are forced to remain in classes so much of the time they are there. Frequent breaks punctuate the elementary school day in Asia; in fact, after every forty- to fifty-minute period there is a recess during which children play vigorously. In contrast to the four or five recesses a day that are typical in Asia, American children often have no more than a single recess. Should we be surprised, therefore, if American children have greater difficulty paying attention than Asian children?

If American children are not motivated to learn, could it be because they live in a society that does not recognize that its schools promote boredom and inattentiveness? Whether or not the discouragement about the nation's children is merited, both teachers and parents need to lure them into situations that will reveal the joys and satisfactions of knowing how to do things well.

If we cannot blame teachers, parents, or students, then who is accountable for the conditions in our schools? The answer is: We are all responsible. We have become accustomed to levels of performance that seemed satisfactory within the context of our own culture but which turn out to be anything but satisfactory compared with that of students from other cultures. Although the United States is among the countries expending the highest proportion of their gross national product on education, our elementary school and secondary school students never place above the median in comparative studies of academic achievement. We have allowed our schools to deteriorate because we failed to attend to what has been going on during the past several decades.

We begin this book with an analysis of cross-cultural differences in academic achievement. We have chosen to emphasize achievement in mathematics both because it is a fundamental subject and because it can be assessed objectively in diverse cultures.

We concentrate throughout the book on young children. The elementary school years are of profound importance not only in themselves, but also in helping us to understand the more complex situations in secondary schools. We also place a special emphasis on the vitality, enthusiasm, and high motivation among Asian children, teachers, and parents, and how they are achieved.

Each of the following chapters focuses on a particular theme in American education that struck us as especially remarkable after studying Japanese and Chinese homes and schools. Many of our conclusions are controversial. Our purpose, however, is to stimulate discussion about the assumptions that underlie the structures and practices of the American educational system. Only through such discussions can our nation hope to reach some consensus about possible solutions to the fundamental problems in American education.

Chapter 2

Academic Achievement

We recently received a letter from a board member of a school district near Boston. "I have been searching for a way to open the eyes of our parents, teachers, administrators, and the general public to the gap between the actual math achievement levels in our schools and the level it takes to be competitive in the world community," the letter began. "So far I have been unsuccessful. Generally, people compare against American benchmarks which indicate 'No problem, we're OK.' Result? People simply do not understand that there is a significant gap, and a widening one."

This impression is in accord with what we have found in our interviews with American parents and children, who express the belief that American students are doing quite well in mathematics. We presented the following situation to several hundred mothers and fathers of Chicago elementary school children: "Let's say that your child took a math test with 100 points. The average score was 70. What score do you think your child would get?" The average score given by mothers was 82, markedly above the average score of 70 for the fictitious test, and only 26 percent of parents gave

28

their children a score of 70 or below. Children echoed the attitudes of their parents. When asked how well they thought they were doing compared to other kids in their class, less than 10 percent rated themselves as below average.

In another set of interviews, with mothers of first-graders and fifth-graders in Minneapolis, we asked each one whether her child had ever had problems with mathematics. Most mothers (i.e., mothers of 90 percent of first-graders and 72 percent of fifth-graders) said their children had never experienced problems.

In short, we have found little evidence that Americans acknowledge the academic weakness of our nation's children. Despite articles in the press and reports in other media, Americans persist in believing that nothing is seriously wrong—that there is no crisis. When they are confronted with data indicating that American children do poorly in academic subjects compared with children in other societies, they dismiss the results and criticize the studies. Even some American scientists, such as Roald Hoffman, the Nobel prizewinner, have questioned whether American children really are behind in their academic achievement. In a column in *The New York Times,* he suggests that "Surveys that plumb the depth of our ignorance and that of our students are methodologically suspect. More importantly, the interpretation of these statistics in isolation is questionable."[1] Others, such as the columnist Jeff Greenfield, express even greater disdain for comparative studies: "Well, here we go again. Once more, for the 3,207th time an Officially Important Survey has revealed that our children are a bunch of morons. This time, the Officially Important Survey reveals, they have been proven a bunch of mathematical morons. And you know what? I don't think I care all that much."[2]

How, in face of this self-satisfaction, are we to persuade Americans that something is indeed wrong? What *is* the evidence that American children do poorly in mathematics? Parents' reactions demonstrate how easy it is to be positive when the only basis for comparison is one's own beliefs about what other American children are doing. Cross-national studies of achievement offer more convincing evidence. In such studies, identical tests are given to large samples of students from different countries, and scores are compared. When these studies are properly conducted, they provide external standards against which we can gauge the achievements of American students.

In this chapter, we compare American children's achievement scores in mathematics and reading with those of Chinese and Japanese children, and then we broaden our focus to ask whether the differences are limited to academic achievement or whether they include more general differences in the ability to handle abstract concepts. Answers to these questions will be central in explaining the performance of American children.

MATHEMATICS

The list of cross-cultural studies of children's academic achievement is short. In mathematics, apart from our own research, there have been two major studies and several smaller ones. The International Association for the Evaluation of Education Achievement conducted the first large-scale study in 1964.[3] The same organization completed a similar study in the early 1980s.[4] Both studies tested the knowledge and skill of eighth-graders and twelfth-graders with a wide variety of mathematical problems, ranging from arithmetic to calculus and number theory.

The general trend of the results was very clear. According to a succinct summary appearing in the National Research Council's report "Everybody Counts":

> Average students in other countries often learn as much mathematics as the best students learn in the United States. Data from the Second International Mathematics Study show that the performance of the top 5 percent of U.S. students is matched by the top 50 percent of students in Japan. Our very best students—the top 1 percent—scored lowest of the top 1 percent in all participating countries.[5]

On no test did American students attain an average score that fell above the median for all of the countries. On tests given to students from twenty countries, American eighth-graders ranked tenth in arithmetic, twelfth in algebra, and sixteenth in geometry. Twelfth-grade American students fared just as badly. When compared to students from fourteen other countries, they were in the lowest quarter in geometry, and in algebra they were second from the bottom.

An even more recent study assessed the mathematical competence of thirteen-year-olds in Korea, Spain, the United Kingdom, Canada, Ireland, and the United States.[6] Students from the United States had the lowest average scores of all the children.

These studies would seem to convey an unmistakable message. Nevertheless, some critics have argued that the results are not as clear as they first appear. For one thing, the percentage of teenagers who are enrolled in high school may vary greatly from country to country, since access to secondary education is not universal. We should not be concerned, the critics suggest, if a representative sample of American students performs more poorly than highly selected groups of students from other countries. We pride ourselves in providing a popular education for all students, and not just an education for a select few.[7] It should be no surprise, therefore, that the more representative American samples obtain lower average scores.

Critics also argue that even when comparisons are based on comparable populations within each country, the results do not give sufficient consideration to differences in the mathematics curricula of different countries. If Japanese high school students do well merely because their courses present topics in greater depth and students are required to take more mathematics courses, this argument runs, we should find little basis for concern. After all, the content of a curriculum is a matter of choice, and such choices often involve tradeoffs among competing goals. We have a diverse society, and we may value many things other than mathematics. According to this argument, American schools are not necessarily at fault; raising scores is simply a matter of reordering priorities so that students are required to spend more time learning mathematics.

A Focus on Children

The critics' alternative interpretations, as well as our desire to understand the genesis of the differences among secondary school students, led us naturally to consider the performance of younger children from different countries. Are cross-cultural differences as striking at the elementary school level as they are among secondary school students? If the answer is yes, then we need to search for deeper interpretations. Differential rates of enrollment in school, for example, could not explain the difference in performance, for elementary school education is compulsory in all industrialized countries.

The first effort to compare mathematics achievement of relatively large samples of elementary school children in different cultures was the study we and our colleagues conducted of Japanese, Chinese, and American elementary school children in 1980.[8] Since then we have completed several other large comparative studies of children's achievement.[9] The results provide consistent and sobering indications of inferior performance by American children. Further, the results dispel any doubt that the poor performance of American high school students could be explained solely by faulty comparisons of subjects or test items.

The studies completed in 1980 and 1987 were similar in basic design. In each we included both first-grade children and fifth-grade children, to give us information about what children knew when they were just entering school as well as after several years of instruction. Rather than attempting to include a large number of cultures, we chose three for intensive study: Chinese, Japanese, and American. Selecting the two Asian cultures was logical because they are among the world's most successful in producing students with high levels of achievement in mathematics. The highest scorers on the second of the international high school mathematics tests were students from Japan and Hong Kong. In advanced algebra, twelfth-graders in Japan and Hong Kong had mean scores of nearly 80 points; that of the American students was a little over 40. Similarly, the mean scores for elementary functions/calculus were over 60 points for the Chinese and Japanese students, but only around 30 points for the American twelfth-graders.

We chose one or two cities within each culture, then sampled schools and children within these cities. Cities in the different cultures were matched as closely as possible for size, economic, and cultural status within their countries.

The settings for the 1980 study were the metropolitan areas of Sendai, Japan, a city 220 miles northeast of Tokyo; Taipei, the capital of the Republic of China (Taiwan); and Minneapolis, Minnesota. The American research site was shifted from Minneapolis to the Chicago metropolitan area in the 1987 study, and Beijing, China, was added as a fourth city.

Falling Far Behind

In tests of mathematics achievement, for both grade levels and in both studies, the scores of American children were far lower than those of their Japanese and Chinese peers.

33

The magnitude of the difference emerges dramatically when we look at the results separately for each of the schools we visited. A graph of the data from our first study appears in Figure 2.2.1, where each point represents the average score of the children in each of the schools included in the study. The scores of the American first-graders and the first-graders from the other cities overlap somewhat. By the fifth grade, however, the groups have diverged. The full range of the population was represented in all of the metropolitan areas sampled, yet even the best American schools were not competitive with their counterparts in Asia on mathematics achievement. The *highest*-scoring American school falls below the *lowest*-scoring Asian schools. These patterns also emerged in the second study, when the research site was shifted from Minneapolis to Chicago (see Figure 2.2.2).

Although American students obviously lag behind Chinese and Japanese students, perhaps the range of students in the United States is greater. Low average scores do not preclude the possibility that the U.S. produces a disproportionate number of very high achievers. To check this possibility, we identified the one hundred students who made the highest scores. In fifth grade, one of these was an American student, eleven were from Taiwan, and eighty-eight were from Japan.

Samples and Tests

These results are dramatic. But we must explain in some detail how we went about conducting the studies, for the power of our findings would be eroded if our procedures were open to serious criticism. Two main questions must be raised: How were the samples of children obtained? How were the samples of items chosen for the tests? If we had not used the same method to select the children in each city, or if we had used test items with cultural biases, it would have been difficult to interpret the findings.

Whom we studied. No cross-national study can be better than the samples of individuals on which it is based. No sampling

FIGURE 2.2
Mathematics achievement for each school
in the 1980 study (2.2.1) and the 1987 study (2.2.2)

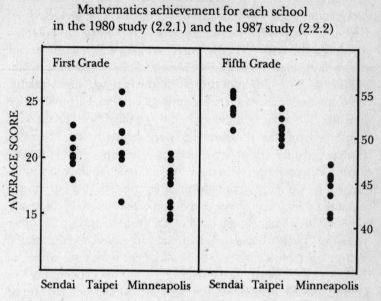

Figure 2.2.1

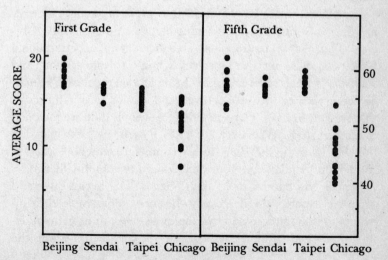

Figure 2.2.2

procedure is perfect, for matters of convenience and cost are always important considerations in any research. Nevertheless, we tried as far as possible to anticipate and minimize the potential sampling problems. We used large samples of children in our studies, and we took great care to select subjects who were representative of the children in the locations where we were working.

No single city can adequately represent a nation. Fortunately, we were able to conduct our research in two quite different American cities, which together do represent a large segment of the American urban population. In our first study, since we suspected that American children might perform poorly compared to their Asian counterparts, we wanted to avoid the possible criticism that our sample contained an unusually large proportion of educationally disadvantaged children. Minneapolis has few of the problems besetting other American cities; it ranks high nationally in indices of educational status, such as students' scores on college entrance tests (where, in 1989, it ranked fourth in the nation), and in the expenditure per pupil at the elementary and secondary levels (where it ranked sixteenth in 1989–90). If children in the Minneapolis metropolitan area performed poorly on our tests, we could expect that children in other large urban areas would be unlikely to fare better.

For our second study we decided to use a markedly different, and in many respects more representative, American city: Chicago. The Chicago metropolitan area includes not only traditional big-city schools, but also inner-city schools, private schools, and suburban schools often praised as being among the nation's finest. Selecting an area with such a diverse population meant, however, that we had to have a larger sample of schools than we included in our first study. Whereas ten schools in each city participated in the 1980 study, in the 1987 study we sampled ten schools each in Taipei and Sendai, eleven in Beijing, and twenty in Chicago.

Sendai was chosen to be our Japanese city because we and Japanese experts considered it to be most comparable to Minneapolis, among representative Japanese cities, in its general demographic and cultural characteristics. Taipei, in 1980, was the only large Chinese city with a traditional Chinese culture that was open to researchers. By the mid-1980s, mainland China had become more open to the West, and it was possible for us to study children in Beijing.

We were careful at each step not to introduce bias into the selection of the children. We relied on local educational authorities and researchers to provide us with information about the schools in each city, and on the basis of their suggestions we were able to select representative samples that included schools in neighborhoods of high, average, and low socioeconomic status. We then randomly chose two first-grade classrooms and two fifth-grade classrooms at each school. The first study included a total of 120 classrooms, and the second, 204.

We are aware that when we speak of "cultures" we are describing what we found in these 324 classrooms in the five large cities included in our studies. We also realize that what we found in Beijing or in Minneapolis does not tell us what we would find in rural Mongolia or in rural Mississippi. What we can say with confidence is that within the cities selected for the studies, the samples of children were chosen in as comparable a manner as possible.

Culture-fair tests. Our research group in the United States, in collaboration with our colleagues in China, Japan, and Taiwan, constructed all the tests used in the research. We undertook this time-consuming and demanding task because we wanted to be sure that the tests were fair and that they covered the knowledge and skills to which the children in each of the cultures had been exposed.

Our first step was to analyze the mathematics textbooks used in each city.[10] In these analyses, we categorized each concept and skill according to the semester and grade in which it was introduced. By comparing the analyses for the different cultures we were able to devise a test that contained the types of items that should have been familiar to children in all three cultures.

37

Testing the children. Children may not do well on tests for many reasons other than lack of knowledge. They may misunderstand the instructions, be unable to read the problems, or lose motivation when the problems start to get difficult. A skilled examiner, giving the tests one-on-one, can anticipate such possibilities and apply the appropriate correctives by being sure the instructions are clear, reading all of the problems aloud to the child, and attempting to maintain the child's interest in the tasks.

With two exceptions, all of the tests in our studies were given in one-on-one sessions, with an examiner testing each child individually. The two exceptions were the computation and geometry tests used in the 1987 study. We sacrificed the advantages of individual testing in these two cases to the goal of obtaining large samples of children. These two tests were administered to whole classrooms at a time. In all, more than seven thousand children took the computation test.

We had to limit the rest of our testing to more reasonable numbers of children, for it was not possible to have one-on-one sessions with thousands of children. We restricted the numbers by randomly selecting subsamples of boys and girls from each classroom.[11] These procedures yielded totals for the two studies, respectively, of 1554 and 1673 first-graders and fifth-graders. These children and their families are the ones who were studied in depth and on whom most of the information in this book was based.

All the cities have compulsory attendance rules for elementary school, and children enter school at roughly the same age in all of the cities. Because testing was scheduled at the equivalent point in the school year in each location, the ages of the children in Taiwan, Japan, and the United States at the time of testing were virtually identical: nearly 6.8 years for the first-graders and nearly eleven years for the fifth-graders. Some children begin school slightly later in Beijing; at the time of testing, the children were several months older than the children in the other cities.

Beyond Computation

One question that might be raised about the data we have presented so far concerns the content of our tests of mathematics achievement. The 1980 test included a combination of computational problems and standard word problems. For the 1987 study, we constructed a battery of tests. The data we have described were from the computation test in this battery.

It is true that computation and word problems represent some of the goals of elementary mathematics curricula, but mathematics educators, and the rest of us, have other goals as well. Children must also understand basic mathematical operations and be able to apply their knowledge creatively. Before we judge the American educational system too hastily, we should be certain that deficiencies demonstrated by American students are not compensated for by strengths in areas more highly indicative of an understanding of the structure and operations of mathematics.

Thus, in addition to testing computational skills in our 1987 study, we also tested children for their understanding of basic mathematical operations, their ability to apply their knowledge to solving meaningful problems, their facility with number concepts, their comprehension of information contained in graphs and tables, their skill in estimation and measurement, and their spatial reasoning abilities. We developed all these tests in consultation with psychologists from each of the cities included in the study and with mathematics educators. The tests covering these areas are described briefly in Table 2.1.

Although some were typical mathematics problems, others were much more novel. Here are some examples:

> Pretend that some Martians came to visit you and they had never heard of addition. If they asked you to tell them all the ways you could use addition, what would you tell them?

> There is a Ferris wheel with four people on it. Point to the person who will be at the highest point in the Ferris wheel

TABLE 2.1

A Brief Description of Tests Used in the 1987 Study

(1)	*Word problems:* Both standard and novel problems were included, some of which were more complex than those found in the textbooks of any of the cultures.
(2)	*Number concepts and equations:* Questions were designed to probe children's understanding of some of the basic number concepts that lie at the foundation of elementary mathematics. Topics included place value, negative numbers, the meaning of equations, and the concept of fractions.
(3)	*Estimation:* Children's ability to map numbers and arithmetical operations onto real-world objects and events was assessed.
(4)	*Operations:* The test measured children's understanding of the basic arithmetical operations, focusing on their ability to explain the uses of the operations and to describe situations in which the operations could be used.
(5)	*Geometry:* Many aspects of basic geometry were included in the test, ranging from vocabulary of geometric terms to problems requiring students to find the area of various regular and irregular two-dimensional figures.
(6)	*Graphing:* Children were asked to extract and use information contained in conventional tabular and graphic representations of data.
(7)	*Visualization and mental folding:* These two tasks assessed visual problem-solving skills that are hypothesized to be important in mathematical problem solving.
(8)	*Mental calculation:* Children were presented with problems that required mental solution of both simple and complex calculations.
(9)	*Oral problems:* First-graders were read statements that assessed, without requiring calculation, their ability to reason about quantity, frequency, ordinal position, and other fundamental mathematical concepts.

after it has gone around three and a half times? (A picture of the Ferris wheel is displayed with the four persons seated at 0, 90, 180, and 270 degrees.)

What two numbers multiplied together would give an answer closest to the target number of 75?: 2, 18, 50, 37.

What is another way to say one half?

Draw a circle around one half the stars. (Two lines containing twelve randomly arranged stars were placed before the child.)

An overview of children's performance on the individual tests, plotted on a common scale, appears in Figure 2.3. It is obvious that the American children's deficiencies in mathematics were pervasive. In nearly every instance the mean scores for the American students were the lowest. The Asian students' superiority was not restricted to a narrow range of well-rehearsed, automatic computational skills, but was manifest across all the tasks. Our data do not support the stereotype of Asian children as successful only in performing what they have learned rather than in applying what they know.

Before First Grade

If cross-cultural differences appear in first grade, would they also be evident even before formal instruction in mathematics begins? To answer this question, we conducted an additional study, in 1984, this time of kindergarten children. If cross-cultural differences were found among kindergarteners, it would be very hard to attribute the poor performance of the older American children solely to their schooling. A full explanation would have to involve the children's homes and their parents.

We visited seventy-two kindergarten classrooms, twenty-four from each city, for this study. All Minneapolis children and nearly all of the Sendai children attend kindergarten; in Taipei, more than 80 percent of the children do so. All children in attendance at the schools were given a mathematics test based on analyses of workbooks from kindergarten and textbooks from first through third grade. We tested children's understanding of such concepts as counting, larger and smaller, place value, ordering, addition, and subtraction. Again, in order to be sure that the children

41

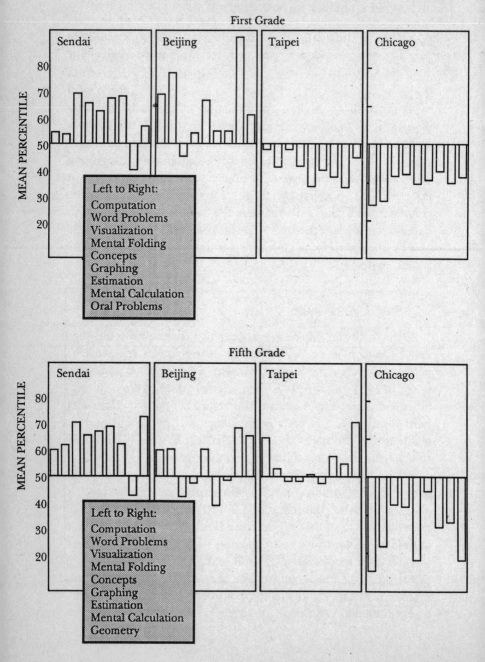

FIGURE 2.3
Children's performance on the battery of mathematics tests in the 1987 study.

understood the questions, we tested each of the nineteen hundred children individually.

As in our earlier results, Japanese children showed consistently superior performance from kindergarten through fifth grade. (For comparative purposes, the data for the first- and fifth-graders from the 1980 study are also graphed in Figure 2.4.) The inferiority of American children compared to Japanese children obviously begins early and grows worse as they pass through elementary school. Chinese children, on the other hand, perform not much better than American children in kindergarten, but show rapid improvement in their scores.

FIGURE 2.4
Children's performance on the mathematics test.

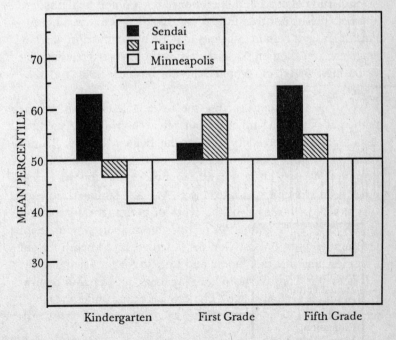

READING

We must next ask whether American children's difficulties are limited to mathematics, or whether they are more widespread and include other subjects, such as reading. There are indications, as we will see, that Americans value reading and literacy much more highly than they do mathematics. Moreover, elementary school students in the United States spend a huge proportion of their school day learning to read—significantly more time than their Asian peers. If American students were to excel in any subject, it is likely that it would be reading.

Comparing reading ability of children in different cultures is a bit more problematic than comparing children's abilities in mathematics. Math has a universal language; the numerals, notation systems, and concepts and operations are common to all modern cultures. This is not true in reading. Languages and writing systems differ, and certain concepts may be represented in one language and not another. Nevertheless, we constructed reading tests with a high degree of comparability for both the 1980 and 1987 studies.

We went about constructing the reading tests as we did the mathematics tests. Members of our research group analyzed the elementary school readers used in the Beijing, Sendai, Taipei, Minneapolis, and Chicago schools, entering each word into a computer, along with its English equivalent and the grade and semester in which it was introduced. We also summarized each story and kept a record of the types of grammatical structures employed at each grade. All of this information was used for devising two tests, one in Chinese, Japanese, and English for our first study, and one in Chinese and English for the second study.

It is easy to construct Chinese, Japanese, and English equivalents of simple sentences like "The kitten is sitting under the table" or "The day we went on a picnic was a cloudy day." These words

44

appear in the textbooks at about the same times, and the syntax is uncomplicated. During the first three elementary school grades, when such simple sentences are likely to appear, the content of the reading tests for the three cultures was identical. In tests in the upper grades, it was impossible to use only identical sentences. American fifth-graders may find a story about the repair of the Statue of Liberty interesting, but such a story is not especially appealing to children in Beijing. Nevertheless, with the careful selection of words of equal levels of difficulty, a comparable story can be written about the repair of a section of the Great Wall. A great deal of time was required for developing these reading tests, but in the end highly reliable estimates of reading and comprehension were developed.

Learning to Read in Three Languages

Any meaningful discussion about comparative reading scores necessarily presumes some knowledge of what is involved in reading English, Chinese, and Japanese. Writing systems based on an alphabet, Chinese characters, and a Japanese syllabary pose different demands on children learning to read.

After Americans learn the alphabet, they must learn how to pronounce the combinations of letters that constitute words. This is not easy, for in English what the reader sees corresponds imperfectly to what he says. Most letters have several pronunciations, depending on the combination of letters in which they appear.

Learning to read Chinese is entirely different. During elementary school, Chinese children must learn approximately three thousand individual characters and the many thousands of words that are formed by combining them. Some researchers believe this task is vastly more difficult than learning to read English; others argue that the irregularities between sounds and spellings make English more difficult to learn to read.

Learning to read Japanese poses still other problems. Four scripts are used in written Japanese: *hiragana,* a cursive script that

45

can be used for writing any Japanese word; *katakana,* an angular script representing the same sounds as *hiragana,* but used most frequently for writing words borrowed from other languages; *kanji,* consisting of Chinese characters and their combinations; and the English alphabet *(romaji),* which is used in scientific notation, titles, and signs.

Which of these three languages poses the most daunting obstacles for beginning readers is a matter of debate. Certainly it is not immediately obvious that English is the most difficult.

Good and Poor Readers

American students tended to be overrepresented among both the best and the worst readers. If children in the three cities perform comparably, approximately thirty-three children from each city should be among those receiving the top one hundred scores. Similarly, there should be approximately thirty-three children from each city among those receiving the lowest one hundred scores. But in our study the number of American children among the worst readers greatly exceeded the number we would expect, if reading skills in the three cities were equivalent. Among first-graders, forty-seven American children were in the bottom group according to their scores on vocabulary tests, and fifty-six American children were in the bottom group in scores measuring their comprehension of what they had read. Corresponding numbers for the fifth-graders were forty-four and forty-seven.

The group of top readers also tended to include a greater number of American children than would be expected. In reading vocabulary, forty-seven American children were among those receiving the top one hundred scores at first grade (although in scores on reading comprehension there were thirty-two American first-graders). The corresponding numbers for fifth-graders were forty and fifty-six.

The trends were repeated in Beijing and Chicago. At both first and fifth grades, a higher percentage of Beijing children were able to read words at their grade level, but more Chicago children were able to read words above their grade level (see Figure 2.5).

The explanation for American students' overrepresentation both below and above their grade level in reading may be related in part to the possibility of breaking down English words by sound. Children who fail to catch on to this possibility tend to be poor readers; children who do learn to break down words by sound are able to read words of high complexity. This characteristic of alphabetic writing systems is not shared by written Chinese or Japanese, where the pronunciation and meaning of characters must be taught and memorized.

Another explanation may be that the division of classrooms in the United States into reading groups gives some students the

FIGURE 2.5

Chinese and American first-graders' ability to read words at and above their grade level.

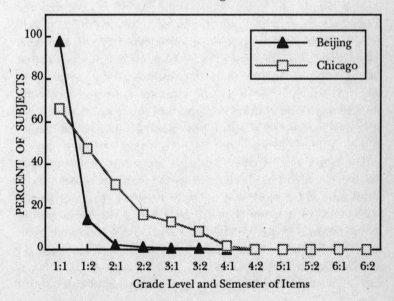

opportunity to learn to read words beyond their grade level. Since all children in Chinese and Japanese classrooms must adhere to the national curriculum, they have little opportunity at school to learn characters at a higher level than the reading curriculum for their grade.

In conclusion, American children do not display exceptional problems in reading achievement. They are, however, overrepresented among the poor readers. A final sobering statistic emphasizes this point: 31 percent of the American fifth-graders, 12 percent of the Chinese, and 21 percent of the Japanese were judged to be reading at the third-grade level—as evidenced by their failure to meet the criterion of reading three fourths of the test items at the fourth-grade level.

THE RETREAT TO GENETICS

Despite the denial by some Americans that our children are lagging behind children in other countries, we believe that our studies, along with the other ones we have described, clearly establish widespread weaknesses in American children's academic achievement. One popular interpretation of these findings is that Asians simply are smarter than Americans. According to this view, superior academic achievement indicates superior underlying abilities to handle abstract concepts and problems. A closely related explanation is that Asians possess some innate skill in mathematics. Neither of these interpretations makes much sense to us.

The claim that Japanese students are more intelligent than American students has been made by the Irish psychologist Richard Lynn, whose work was publicized several years ago in the cover story of a national magazine.[12] Using American norms, Lynn computed Japanese children's scores on a commonly used test of intelligence. On this scale, Japanese children's average IQ was significantly above the American average. Lynn's claims, if correct, would add greatly to our understanding of cultural differences in achievement, but as another publication has pointed out, they are wrong.[13] Asian children may learn more during their school years, but their *capacity* for learning—which is what intelligence tests attempt to measure—does not differ from that of American children.

The fundamental flaw in Lynn's report was his failure to consider two important variables: location of residence (urban versus rural) and socioeconomic status of the children's families. One of the consistent findings since intelligence tests were devised nearly a century ago has been the large differences between IQ scores of city children and children living in remote villages, and between children from upper-income families and from disadvantaged homes. Lynn did not gather any of his information himself, but instead relied on the norms of the test that were published in the test manual. His choice was unfortunate. Because intelligence tests in Japan are used primarily in large cities, only urban children had been tested to establish the norms. Moreover, no attention had been paid to the necessity of selecting a representative sample of children from each Japanese city. The norms for the American test, by contrast, were based on a truly representative sample of urban and rural children of all socioeconomic levels.

We can do more than criticize Lynn's methodology. Data we obtained from an intelligence test given to the children in our 1980 study contradict his claims. The test, constructed especially for use in Japan, Taiwan, and the United States, included items tapping the children's vocabulary, general information, memory, spatial, and perceptual skills, ability to use a code, and so on—all topics not explicitly taught in school. As with the mathematics tests, we developed these items with a team of researchers from each of the cultures.

Contrary to what would be expected if cross-cultural differences in general intelligence could explain the striking differences in achievement, we found little overall difference in the levels of cognitive functioning of children across the three cultures.[14] American children did not display lower intellectual abilities than

Chinese and Japanese children. Scores for the individual children from each culture on the different types of items were not identical, but by the fifth grade the scores for the total test did not differ significantly from one culture to another. Children in each culture displayed slightly different cognitive strengths and weaknesses, but by the time they were enrolled in the fifth grade, the most notable feature was the similarity of their performance.

DEFINING THE PROBLEM

A close examination of American children's academic achievement rapidly dispels any notion that we face a problem of limited scope. The problem is not restricted to a certain age level or to a particular academic subject. Whether we look at the average scores for schools or at the scores for individuals, we find evidence of serious and pervasive weakness. In mathematics, the weakness is not limited to inadequate mastery of routine operations, but reflects a poor understanding of how to use mathematics in solving meaningful problems. Nor is mathematics the only subject in which American students do poorly. We have presented evidence of the overrepresentation of poor readers among American children, and American students have fared badly in international studies of achievement in science.

The hypothesis that the academic weakness of American children is due to deficiencies in innate intellectual ability is without merit. American children obtained scores highly similar to those of the Asian children on a culturally fair test of intelligence, and we have found no sound evidence that American children's academic problems stem from a deficiency in handling abstract concepts.

Similarly, we see no substantial basis for positing differences among the races in innate mathematical ability. How could a genetic hypothesis account for the remarkable improvement shown by children in Taiwan between kindergarten and fifth grade? During kindergarten their scores were little better than those of American children; by fifth grade the Chinese children had greatly surpassed them. Moreover, American children's shortcomings are not limited to mathematics. Would lack of specific innate abilities also be posited to account for low scores in tests of reading, geography, or science?

The puzzle lies in trying to understand the poor performance of American children. If explanations that rely on innate endowment are unsatisfactory, then we must look to children's everyday experiences. The most likely locales are those where children spend most of their time: home and school. Just as cross-cultural comparisons help to expose the academic weaknesses of U.S. children, so should such comparisons help to identify those aspects of American homes and schools that contribute to poor academic performance.

Chapter 3

Children's Lives

Families, schools, and wider cultural beliefs all play a part in children's academic successes and failures. Yet all of these factors are ultimately effective only through the influence they have on the daily lives of individual children.

If we described only the contexts and activities experienced by a Chicago or a Minneapolis child, they would be more or less familiar to all of us, either from our own memories of elementary school or from the experiences of our children or those of our friends. But if we contrast the daily life of an American child with that of a typical Chinese or Japanese child, the familiar events of American childhood take on new meaning.

HOME AND SCHOOL

The way young children divide their day between home and school tells us something about the emphasis societies place on schooling. American children spend less time in academic activities than Chinese and Japanese children do measured in terms of hours spent at school each day and days spent in school each year.

American children are at school approximately six hours each weekday. Only first-graders in Asia spend so little time at school. In Beijing, as in Sendai and Taipei, children from second grade on are at school more than eight hours every weekday, and they return for four hours of classes on Saturday. These hours are not taken up solely by formal classes, however, for most children participate in after-school activities, which range from sewing and calligraphy to the martial arts and electronics, depending on the resources of the school. School continues throughout the year for Chinese and Japanese children, broken by several vacations—six or seven weeks in the summer, several weeks in early winter, a few weeks in fall and spring.

American children spend about half the days of each year in school; Chinese and Japanese children spend two thirds. Even during their vacations, Chinese and Japanese children never really lose contact with their teachers or schoolmates. School activities merge into home activities more naturally when the year is not divided into two sharply defined segments and when, as happens in Asia, the same teacher remains with a class for at least two years. The smooth flow of school attendance throughout the year produces a very different relationship between home and school from that created in the United States, where there is a complete break during several months of summer vacation, and where next fall's teacher will be new.

LIFE AT HOME

The best way to find out how children spend their time outside school would be to follow them around for several days and observe where they go and what they do. Following hundreds of children around after school was impossible for us; so we asked their mothers to supply this information for a weekday and for the

Saturday and Sunday preceding our interview with them. From the mothers' replies, we constructed a weekly estimate of how the children spent their time, divided between activities that were related to school and those that were not.[1]

Academic Activities at Home

Most Asian students appear to see school as central to their lives; most American students do not. As a result, Asian children spend vastly more time at home on schoolwork than do American children. Asian parents support their children's efforts by organizing the home environment to make it conducive to studying.

Most homes are not natural settings for academic activities; it takes effort to provide children with the space and materials necessary for doing their schoolwork. Generally, Asian parents have gone much further than American parents in making their homes suitable for studying. Providing children with a room or quiet space comes at noticeable cost to most Asian families, who have little space in their cramped apartments for anything but the essentials for everyday living. The typical Japanese family occupies less than nine hundred square feet of space in what are sometimes derided as "rabbit hutches." Nevertheless, more than 80 percent of families in Japan and Taiwan set aside space where their children can do their schoolwork.

In addition to allocating space for studying, Chinese and Japanese parents also purchase a very important item: a desk. Whereas more than 95 percent of Taipei parents and 98 percent of Sendai parents had bought their fifth-graders a desk, only 63 percent of Minneapolis parents of fifth-graders had done so. Even as early as first grade, more than 80 percent of the Taipei and Sendai children had their own desks.

The desks purchased by Japanese parents tend not to be simple tables; they are expensive, efficient units with shelves, drawers, and lights. In Beijing, where few families are allotted more than a couple of rooms, it is unlikely that there would be space in most apartments for a child's desk. After dinner is over, however, the dining table is cleared so that the children have a place to study.

By providing space and a personal desk, parents not only make it easier for their children to study, they also convey the message that they consider studying to be important. Children may feel, in turn, that they must justify the family's sacrifices by devoting themselves appropriately to their schoolwork. In one home we occasionally visited in Taiwan we often found the father, a businessman, doing his office work on a tiny couch in the middle of the living room. Although he had no desk at home for himself, each of his two elementary school children had desks. If there is a desk in American homes, it is more likely to belong to a parent than to a child.

Homework. Asian teachers assign large amounts of homework, and Asian children devote significant portions of their time to getting it done. Large cross-cultural differences were evident as early as the first grade. Mothers' estimates of the time spent on homework by Sendai first-graders were three times as high, and for Taipei children, seven times as high, as those for Minneapolis children. Beijing first-graders spent more than twice as much time doing homework as the Chicago first-graders, despite the fact that the Chicago Board of Education had imposed a requirement of a minimum of thirty minutes a day of homework for the first three grades. At the fifth grade, discrepancies among children in Taipei, Sendai, and Minneapolis were equally dramatic. Fifth-graders in Minneapolis spent slightly more than four hours a week on homework—significantly less than the six hours in Sendai and a vastly smaller amount of time than the thirteen hours in Taipei. The effect of the homework requirement in Chicago—forty-five minutes for grades four through six—became evident by the fifth grade, when the amount of time spent by Chicago and Beijing children differed by only an hour a week.

Homework is assigned to Asian children not only during the school year, but during the rest of the year as well. For example, all Taipei teachers said they gave their pupils homework to complete during the winter vacation, which corresponds to the American Christmas vacation. Only 12 percent of the Minneapolis teachers gave such assignments. Similarly, two thirds of the Japanese teachers said that they made homework assignments for the six-week summer break. American children would find it inconceivable to be expected to spend part of their summer vacation doing homework.

Workbooks. In addition to homework assigned by their teachers, Chinese and Japanese children are also more likely than American children to spend time at home with workbooks created to review and supplement their regular textbooks. More than 60 percent of the mothers of fifth-graders in Taipei and Sendai, but only 41 percent of the mothers in Minneapolis, had purchased workbooks for their children.

It is not easy for American parents to find good workbooks. They are sometimes available near check-out counters in grocery stores and at some bookstores, but there is little variety, and their content is generally dull and unimaginative. Japanese and Taiwanese parents are more fortunate. In the typical Sendai bookstore, for example, colorful, cleverly illustrated workbooks, packed with thoughtful material presented in the form of exercises, games, and puzzles, fill row after row. Rather than requiring repetition of simple facts and operations, Japanese and Chinese workbooks are useful supplements to what the children are learning in school. The most frequently purchased workbooks in all cities were for reading and mathematics, but there was a startling difference in the percentages of families purchasing science workbooks: 2 percent in Minneapolis, 52 percent in Taipei, and 41 percent in Sendai.

The costs of studying. Despite the fact that Asian children spend long hours studying, they did not impress us as being especially tense or anxious. The situation may be different in

Asian high schools, where studying for entrance examinations becomes an all-consuming goal, but in our studies of elementary school children we found no evidence that the emphasis on schoolwork took a psychological toll. Neither Chinese nor Japanese elementary school children displayed any greater frequency of psychological problems than did American children. In fact, American teachers reported a greater frequency of inattentiveness, hyperactivity, and student complaints of headaches, stomachaches, and not wanting to come to school than did Chinese teachers. If anything, Asian children's frank enthusiasm about school (to be described later) would suggest that studying hard may lead to a feeling of accomplishment and mastery that actually enhances their self-image and their adjustment to school.

Leisure Activities at Home

When we look at children's leisure-time activities, we see differences, but few dramatic disparities, among the cultures. Contrary to critics' claims, American children do not spend inordinate amounts of after-school time watching television or playing. Asian children do spend more time than American children reading for pleasure, and American children spend more time doing chores, but the children appear to be leading balanced lives. All of the societies seem to have happy, energetic, and enthusiastic youngsters. Nowhere did we observe the image often projected in the American media of intensely competitive, overworked, single-minded Asian children who outdo their American peers by forgoing the pleasures of childhood for the rewards of academic success.

Play. Playing and watching television are the two activities unrelated to school that occupy the largest portions of children's time at home. It is in the first of these activities that children in the various cities differed the most. In both Minneapolis and Chicago, fifth-graders played an average of over two hours a day after school. Children in Sendai played an average of an hour and a half per day. In contrast, Taipei mothers estimated that their fifth-graders played a little more than half an hour a day. In addition to play, American fifth-graders also spent more time on organized sports than did the children in Asia. For example, Chicago children spent an average of four hours a week on sports, compared to three hours for children in Beijing.

We were surprised when we first calculated how much time American children spent in play and on sports—more than twenty-six hours a week when weekends are included. But when we looked further at the children's daily schedules, we began to understand why American children may actually need so much time for physical activity and social interaction. As we will see, their opportunities at school for playing and interacting with other children are far more restricted than in Asian schools.

Television. Social critics deplore at length the hours American children spend in front of the television set. Actually, mothers' estimates of the time their fifth-graders watched television indicated that the Japanese children watched as much, if not more, television each day as American children: 2.0 in Japan versus 1.8 hours a day in the United States. In turn, American children watched more television than the children in Taipei or Beijing. Limited programming on Chinese television, especially for children, reduced television viewing in Beijing to about an hour a day.

Critics also like to suggest that Japan and other countries must have better television programming than the United States does, but we see no evidence that this is true. Commercial television's mix of educational and entertainment programs appears to be much the same in all three locations. An overdose of *yakusa*, *samurai*, or Godzilla movies is probably as dulling to children in Japan as G.I. Joe, Ninja Turtle, or Chip 'n' Dale's Rescue Rangers programs are in the United States.

The difference among the cultures may lie in the conditions parents impose on television viewing. Chinese and Japanese parents are more likely than American parents to make television viewing dependent on the completion of homework. Instead of being displaced by television viewing, homework takes precedence over it.

Reading. Children in Sendai are the most avid readers. They are estimated to spend 5.7 hours per week reading for pleasure, compared with 4.3 hours in Taipei and 3.8 hours in Minneapolis. Similarly, Beijing children read more than Chicago children: an hour a week more at first grade, and two hours a week at fifth grade.

What children read depends in part on the availability of reading materials. Metropolitan newspapers in the United States do not publish special pages with articles written for children of different ages, as they commonly do in Asian cities. In addition to children's pages in newspapers for adults, special newspapers are published for children in Taiwan. As a result, more than half of the Taipei elementary school children read newspapers, compared to nearly one third in Sendai and one fourth in Minneapolis.

In Japan, children's magazines are very popular, and families typically subscribe to at least one of them. Some magazines contain only stories; others include games and quizzes, and often there are inserts of special items, such as puzzles or miniature objects that can be assembled. In front of most Japanese bookstores are metal stands displaying an array of colorful children's magazines, with special editions for each grade level. Among these are thick comic books, which have become popular in both Taiwan and Japan. Some consist primarily of drawings with minimal text; others contain the texts of Chinese and Japanese classics. Although some excellent children's magazines are published in the United States, such as *Cricket, Ranger Rick,* and *Highlights for Children,* they have never achieved the popularity of children's magazines in Japan.

Beijing children read books. In Beijing, small paperbacks costing about twenty cents each are widely available, and children own a surprisingly large number of them. Our data showed that the Beijing children owned an average of one hundred fourteen books; Chicago children owned an average of sixty-seven. The difference may be due, in part, to the wider availability of books in school and public libraries in the United States.

Helping around the house is another after-school activity. American children tend to do more chores than children in Asia. By the fifth grade, Chicago children were spending 50 percent more time doing chores than the children in Beijing: four and one half hours versus three hours a week. Minneapolis children also did more household chores than the children in Sendai and Taipei. In fact, 93 percent of the Minneapolis children were assigned chores, compared to three fourths of the Sendai children and only a quarter of the Taipei children.

Perhaps there is less need for help in the small living quarters of most Asian families; a more likely reason for Asian children's spending less time on chores is the Asian parents' desire that children spend as much time as possible on their studies. This attitude was clearly expressed by one of the Taipei mothers, who explained why her child did not do chores: "My child is too busy. All she has to do is her duty as a student." American mothers gave other reasons why they assigned their children chores. Some emphasized the benefit to the child ("it instills a sense of responsibility," "helps the child learn organization," "teaches good habits"). Others explained their assignment of chores as being helpful to the family ("everyone in the family must contribute to the benefit of the whole family," "it contributes to the household," and "it's a job that needs to be done." Rarely did an American mother mention anything related to school when asked to explain why her child did not do chores.

The day at home. We have summarized the data about children's lives at home in Table 3.1 below. It is evident that Asian children spend much more time on activities related to their schoolwork than do American children. Such activities are em-

TABLE 3.1
Average Number of Hours Per Weekday Children
in Three Cities Spend in Various Activities

Activity	Sendai	Taipei	Minneapolis
School	6.5	8.3	6.0
Homework	1.0	1.9	.8
Play	1.5	.6	2.4
Television	2.0	1.2	1.8
Reading	.9	.7	.6
Sleep	9.3	8.8	10.0
Other	2.8	2.5	2.4

phasized and supported within Chinese and Japanese families from the children's first days of school. By the later years of elementary school it is expected that children will devote several hours of after-school time to academic activities. It is not surprising that the extra practice resulting from hours of homework, reading, and filling in workbooks should help the children's progress in school. Everyone knows that learning to read and do mathematics, like swimming and baseball, requires time and practice. But American families are not enthusiastic about having their children dedicate much of their free time to schoolwork. Indeed, when our Japanese colleagues heard about how little time American children spend on studying and reading, they expressed great admiration for American children. How could they do as well as they do when they read and study so little at home and spend so little time at school?

THE DAY AT SCHOOL

It is much easier to observe children's activities at school than it is to follow them around after they leave school. We have been able, through literally hundreds of hours of observation in classrooms, to construct a detailed picture of what goes on in the elementary schools of the five cities. From the organization of the school day to the content and sequence of lessons, children's experiences in Asian schools are highly planned, much more so than in American schools. This we expected. What we did not appreciate before we began our research is how strongly oriented Asian schools are toward promoting social interaction among the children.

Maintaining Order in the Classroom

The Asian teacher faces a very different set of demands from those faced in the American classroom. Dealing with thirty-eight to fifty children, with no tracking or separation according to their level of ability, imposes a strong need on the teacher to create order and structure. This is accomplished in several ways.

First, teachers make an explicit effort during the early months of elementary school to teach children techniques and skills that will allow them to function effectively in a group. Children learn how to move from one activity to another, how to arrange the contents of their desks so that they can find things easily, how to pay attention, how to follow directions, and how to speak loudly and clearly so that they can be understood. By equipping children with these skills, Asian teachers are able to handle large classes in a smooth and unflustered manner. Children's easy transitions from one activity to another and their readiness to carry out classroom routines occur not because Asian children are docile or passive, but because they have been taught efficient and useful ways of handling themselves in the classroom. Asian teachers are willing to take the time to teach these skills because, among other reasons, they know they will reap the benefits for more than a single year. The same group of children will remain with the teacher for two years, or sometimes even three or more.

A second factor contributing to the calm orderliness of the

Asian classroom is that classroom discipline is not considered the responsibility of the teacher alone, but is shared with the children themselves. Children are given responsibilities for managing the classroom that far exceed those in most American elementary schools. The burden for maintaining discipline is shifted from the teacher to the children themselves, and especially to the child who is currently functioning as class leader. Because each child knows that he will eventually be responsible for maintaining class discipline, he is more ready to follow the suggestions of the day's leader.

The sense of responsibility for discipline is part of a broader obligation on the part of children to assist in the daily functioning of the school. There are few janitors in Chinese and Japanese schools. The children are responsible for cleaning the desks, sweeping and scrubbing the floors, emptying wastebaskets, and washing the blackboards. There are no graffiti on the walls, because the children know that they will be responsible for removing them. Nor are there cafeterias in most Japanese elementary schools. Food is brought to the classroom to be served by the children, who are also responsible for the after-lunch cleanup. There is no horseplay during lunch; whatever is spilled or messed up will only require additional cleanup by the class. Participation in these activities obviously helps the school maintain order and cleanliness, but perhaps even more important, it contributes to the students' sense of responsibility for the school and identification with it.

Loneliness in the Classroom

Perhaps the most profound difference in the way Asian and American children spend their time at school is in the degree to which they are alone versus being part of a group. American children have far fewer opportunities for group participation than do Chinese and Japanese children. The difference begins when they don their backpacks and leave for school. When schools are near the children's homes, as they are in most Chinese and Japanese cities, children walk to school. Children in metropolitan areas in the United States more commonly take a bus that arrives at school very shortly before the opening bell and leaves very soon after the day's session is over. Many American children not only spend little time at school either before or after their classes are over, but also are less likely to have time for leisurely social interaction with their schoolmates as they go to school or return home.

American children also spend much of their school day in the classroom. Some Chicago schools had no recesses at all, and the average was less than one a day. None of the Minneapolis schools had more than two recesses a day. In striking contrast, every academic class period in Chinese and Japanese schools was followed by a recess. Children in the Beijing schools had an average of four or five ten- to fifteen-minute recesses a day; in Taipei, four; and in Sendai, five. During these recess periods, children go outside for vigorous play at Ping-Pong, hopscotch, badminton, jump rope, basketball, and other games. Children are noisy, active, energetic, and interactive. These opportunities are limited for the urban American child, except for the hour devoted to physical education several times a week and a short time each day for playground activities.

The greater opportunity for Chinese and Japanese children to play during school hours may result in less need to play after school, and it also may be an important factor in explaining their academic performance. Western visitors to Asian classrooms often comment on the children's rapt attention. Their ability to focus so closely on academic activities may be due partly to their frequent opportunities during recesses to relax, socialize, and escape from the demands of the classroom. American children must wait; only after school is over do they have time to play and thereby to reduce the tensions created by sitting in the classroom.

Even more important than these nonacademic activities is the way in which time is organized within the classroom. A major division is between seatwork, where children work on assignments alone at their desks, and activities that involve the whole class. According to our observations, Chicago children spend a great deal of time working on their own. The time spent at their desks filling in workbooks or handout sheets, reading, and doing other solitary activities occupied nearly 50 percent of their class time, but never more than 31 percent of the class time in the Asian cities. Conversely, Sendai, Beijing, and Taipei children spent most of their time in classrooms that were organized so that all of the children were working as a unit with the teacher as leader. Participation in lessons that involve the whole class, even in classes with many students, enhances students' feelings of group membership and reduces their sense of isolation.

Several of the American mothers we interviewed expressed approval of the fact that their child's teacher allowed the children to work at their own pace. This practice may have benefits, but working at one's own pace means working alone, and the slower one's pace, the more time spent alone. Many times we observed a class where all but a few of the children had finished their assignment. The remaining few children struggled alone. Although they weren't being hurried, they were paying the price of slowness by being deprived of the extra time for social interaction that went to those who finished early.

When small groups are formed in Chinese and Japanese classrooms, children are selected so that all levels of achievement as well as other characteristics will be represented in each group. In Japan, these groups are known as *han*. Members of the *han* operate as a unit, and its rate of progress, access to privileges, and social acknowledgments depend on the group's activities rather than on those of any individual. The mutual support that exists within the *han* is very effective in promoting the feeling of group membership. Children function on an equal footing, but it is acknowledged that each child will not always contribute equally to the *han*'s progress.

One Japanese teacher explained to us her method of grouping children: "I mix the groups so that each child has something to contribute. Each group should have a top student, but it would not be good to put all of the top students together. A group needs other talents as well: someone with artistic talents, someone who is good at sports, and so on."

In one classroom we observed the results of this kind of planning. The children were preparing group presentations relevant to the day's social studies topic. Within each *han*, different children exercised leadership based on their particular skills. We could identify one child who had apparently organized her group's presentation; another who was adept at making posters; and another, presumably the group's expert at public speaking, who eventually walked to the front and, in a loud clear voice, presented the group's report. Participation in groups such as this enables children to learn to judge each other by multiple yardsticks, and to come to appreciate the variety of ways individuals can contribute to a group's success.

Involvement in such different modes of classroom organization day after day, year after year, seems likely to enhance the individualism of the American child and the group orientation of the Chinese and Japanese child. As a result of American children's more limited opportunities for group interaction and classroom participation, there appears to be a greater loneliness among them. We understood why American children are more likely to seek other children for after-school play, why they spend so much time in their classrooms talking inappropriately to other children, and why they might not find school an especially pleasant place to be. Indeed, American children are less likely than Chinese or Japanese children to say they like school. For example, between 75 percent and 86 percent of the children in Taipei, compared to between 52 percent and 65 percent of the American children (depending on the grade and study) indicated that they liked school. Similarly, 94 percent of the children in Beijing and only 78 percent of the children in Chicago said that they liked school. Beijing children indicated their positive feelings about school in several other ways. Compared to the Chicago children, they were more eager to go to school in the mornings (94 percent versus 65 percent), talked more positively about school (84 percent versus 67 percent), and even expressed an eagerness for their vacations to end so they could return to school (66 percent versus 27 percent).

Cram Schools

Although Asian elementary school children spend more hours at school than American children, they do not attend after-school academic classes with any great frequency. A great deal has been written about the long school day in Asia resulting from attendance at after-school "cram schools"—called *buxiban* in Taiwan and *juku* in Japan. Both are private schools that offer special classes, including academic classes such as mathematics and nonacademic classes such as calligraphy. But academically oriented cram schools mainly prepare high school students for college entrance examinations; elementary school children spend little time at them. In Taipei, only 2 percent of the first-graders and 14 percent of the fifth-graders in our study attended such classes or had a tutor for academic subjects. The percentages were higher among Japanese children; 16 percent of the first-graders and 46 percent of the fifth-graders attended *juku*, but few of them studied academic subjects. Japanese children tended to study English or the operation of the abacus, and only 10 percent of the fifth-graders studied mathematics. Fewer than 6 percent of the Chinese children studied either reading or mathematics.

DEFINING THE PROBLEM

Americans often attribute the problems with their schools to poor physical facilities and excessive numbers of students. Our data, especially from Taiwan and China, go a long way toward dispelling such interpretations. Large schools, large class size, and old-fashioned school buildings do not necessarily limit children's academic achievement. Large classes can be managed effectively if the teachers are not overworked, if students are attentive, and if time and energy are not wasted in inefficient transitions from one activity to another and in irrelevant activities. Modern school plants may be more comfortable than older ones, but they offer no assurance that children will learn more effectively.

Nor can we explain low achievement, at least during the elementary school years, by the amount of time children spend after school watching television and playing. There is not a close correspondence among the different cities between children's academic achievement and the amount of time they spend viewing television. Similarly, the amount of time children spend in play offers little insight into the bases of academic achievement. What does seem to be important is the way these leisure-time activities are managed. Chinese and Japanese children know that they will have free time only after they have completed the day's schoolwork. In American families, leisure activities and schoolwork compete for the child's time.

A notable characteristic of the lives of American children is a striking discontinuity between home and school. This is evident in the meager amount of time children spend after school on academically oriented activities, such as doing homework, using workbooks, and reading for pleasure. Americans accept the need for practice and drill to achieve excellence in sports, music, or dance, but few parents—and even fewer children—favor spending more time at home on academic activities. Their distaste for schoolwork poses a serious problem. Daily lessons cannot be mastered without review and practice, and American students cannot gain this experience as long as teachers are reluctant to increase the amount of homework and parents and children hold unfavorable views about its value. Americans have some justification for their negative attitudes; homework assignments and workbooks for American children are often criticized as shallow, boring, and repetitious. Providing children with organized and meaningful assignments takes time, and most American teachers do not have sufficient time to devote to this activity. (The issue of teaching hours and nonteaching time is discussed in Chapter 8.)

Because Chinese and Japanese families believe their children's primary responsibility is to apply themselves seriously to their schoolwork, they arrange their home life so that it is conducive to academic activities. For American children, what happens at school often has little relation to what happens at home. It is paradoxical that so many American parents pay little attention to providing an inviting environment for studying at home, even though they are convinced that the physical conditions at school are important to their children's education. The priorities American families assign to their household purchases send a clear message about what they value. A child's desk is rarely at the top of the list.

The way American children spend their days at school further impedes high academic achievement. Americans emphasize individuality, an emphasis that has both emotional and academic costs for children. Teachers often leave children to work alone at their desks, and frequently divide the class into small groups, separated according to the children's level of skill. Teachers spend a good deal of time working with these groups and with individual children, and the class operates as a whole only part of the time. So each child spends relatively little time in direct interaction with the teacher. Children spend most of the school day in the classroom, with little time for play and social interaction. As a result, one senses that American children often feel isolated and lonely. Partly for this reason, they are less enthusiastic about school than their Chinese and Japanese peers. Until the school day is reorganized so that there is time for more than six subjects and a fast lunch, it is unlikely that school will assume a central place in the lives of American children.

Working alone a large part of the time may also contribute to the American children's lower levels of academic achievement. Although children can learn without a teacher's direct attention, it seems unlikely that independent activity is the most effective means of instruction. One might argue that skill in a subject such as reading is highly dependent on practice and that children benefit from reading by themselves. It is more difficult to summon this argument for mathematics or science, where more information and demonstrations about definitions and operations may be necessary before children are ready to practice on their own. What appears to be a devotion to individuals and to small groups of children has the unintended effect of removing the American teacher from the remaining children and depriving those children of valuable opportunities for instruction. We delude ourselves when we recommend individualizing instruction under the conditions that exist in American elementary schools. Teachers cannot possibly work individually and effectively during regular class periods with all of the children who need help.

The whole-class instruction that typifies Asian classrooms might be expected to result in regimentation and conformity. It does not. Visitors to Chinese and Japanese elementary schools are struck by the children's apparent pleasure and involvement in schoolwork. Classes operate smoothly and efficiently, but not in a rigid, authoritarian fashion. Achieving such efficiency and still meeting the needs of individual children is the result of careful planning and training. Children are taught classroom routines and social skills, and the schedule allows time for relaxation and social interaction. As a result, Chinese and Japanese elementary schools not only promote learning, they also are places that children enjoy.

Asian elementary school classrooms are not highly competitive. Children are eager to display what they know, and they are challenged to learn what is being taught rather than to surpass other children. One of the secrets of Asian schooling is the strong identification pupils feel with each other and with the school. Orderliness and discipline come to be imposed by the children on one another, rather than by adult authorities. Children learn how to handle themselves in groups and, at the same time, learn how to manage children who are disturbing the group's operation. Above all, children gradually develop self-direction, good study habits, and motivation to do well in school. "When I was begin-ning school," said one Chinese student, "my parents always asked me if I'd done my homework. But after that, I wanted to do well in school because of my own interest and the challenge involved in learning. What am I doing it for, except for myself?" Because most Asian children understand why studying is important, their devotion to their schoolwork gives them a feeling of competence rather than a feeling that school is a source of tension, anxiety, or boredom.

The ideal day in the lives of elementary school children bal-ances physical, social, and intellectual activity, allows children opportunities for gaining a sense of accomplishment and compe-tence, has both structure and freedom, and gradually evolves—so that what is expected of children follows their developmental progress. We must ask whether Americans are as successful in providing their children opportunities for approaching these goals as parents and teachers are in Chinese and Japanese societies.

Chapter 4

Socialization and Achievement

What makes children want to work hard, be excited about school, and see school as a place they want to be? How do adults transmit positive values about school to children? To answer these questions we need to examine at least three issues.

The first is timing: When must adults intervene to ensure that children will adopt the beliefs and attitudes that will lead them to value academic achievement? The second issue is the contributions of parents and of teachers to this process: How can parents and teachers help make school an exciting place for children? The final issue is technique: What methods are effective in motivating children? The positions adults take on these issues, whether consciously or unconsciously, strongly influence how children are socialized to want to be effective students.

As with any complex phenomenon, views on this topic vary considerably within our society. Even so, extensive interviews with parents and teachers in the United States reveal that Americans do share an implicit model of socialization. They generally believe that in order to excel in elementary school, children must be given a head start by their parents and preschool teachers. Americans also tend to assume that Asian parents adopt a similar approach, and to attribute Asian students' academic excellence primarily to the intensity of this approach.

The interviews we conducted in Japan, Taiwan, and China suggest that this assumption is wrong. Chinese and Japanese parents, although not identical in their approaches to child-rearing, do share beliefs about children's socialization that differ radically from those held by American parents. As we will see, these contrasting beliefs lead to sharply differing practices.

Chinese and Japanese parents make an important distinction between early and later childhood, and they engage in different socialization practices with children at these different ages. Until their children are about six years old, Asian parents impose few demands or controls on them. They believe that this is a period when children should learn how to relate to others, and there is little pressure to learn academic skills. About the time children enter first grade, child-rearing practices shift markedly, and parents and children begin to work diligently on what is defined as the primary task of later childhood and youth: getting a good education.

American parents, in contrast, do not noticeably alter their child-rearing practices according to a child's age. Parents often begin to work on academic skills early in the child's life and expect kindergarten teachers to help them. The goals of socialization do not change greatly when their children enter first grade, but the agent responsible for academic socialization does change. Just when Asian parents are getting more involved in their children's academic life, American parents are beginning to abdicate many of their responsibilities to their children's teachers.

THE AGE OF INNOCENCE

According to Chinese conceptions, childhood is divided into two periods, one sometimes described as the age of innocence— usually considered to encompass the child's first six years—followed by a stage known as the age of reason. The age of innocence is considered to be a time for indulgence by adults—a period of great freedom and an opportunity for exploration. Because young children are assumed to lack cognitive competence, adults make few attempts to teach them academic skills, abstract concepts, or even morality. Then when they enter elementary school, children are expected to begin the transformation into intellectual beings capable of learning the rules of social life and the content of the school curriculum. Parental expectations change accordingly. Actions that were acceptable during the age of innocence often meet with disapproval when the child enters the age of reason.

The Japanese hold a similar conception of these two periods. "We think of young children as angels who are visiting this life," our Japanese colleague Hiroshi Azuma says. "We believe we must treat them with great love and affection if we are to convince them to stay with us, rather than returning to heaven." Once the children have demonstrated their satisfaction with this world, by the age of six or so, parents become more demanding, setting their sights on the serious business of school.

Lois Peak, an American researcher, tells an interesting story about her efforts to understand the early roots of Japanese children's academic achievement. Expecting to find some of the secrets of Japanese academic success in children's early home environments, she decided to observe Japanese preschoolers in their homes. After several months of observation, she came up empty-handed: Japanese mothers were not greatly concerned with training their children to be students. In fact, they were puzzled when Peak described the purpose of her study. "If you want to know how children become good students, why are you observing in homes?" they asked. "Why don't you observe in schools?"

Americans are surprised to learn that the achievements of Japanese children are not accompanied by a more task-oriented life at home. In fact, it is the American parents who hold more strongly to the belief that they must begin early to further their children's intellectual development. American parents hold varying views, but generally think of the young child as a slate on which they had better begin writing as soon as possible if the child is to compete in the difficult outside world. There is a strong belief in the importance of early experience for cognitive development and in the long-term negative effects of a lack of early cognitive stimulation. American parents have little patience with those who consider young children as angels, as innocents who are to be indulged. Instead, they appear to believe that even the youngest child can benefit from appropriate cognitive stimulation, and they strive to supply children with experiences that will stimulate them.

American parents purchase mobiles to hang above their babies' cribs to stimulate visual development, infant scooters to hasten motor development and exploration, and puzzle boxes to encourage the development of curiosity. They begin reading to their children at an early age. Among American mothers of the kindergarteners we studied, 91 percent reported reading to their preschool children daily or several times a week. Only 40 percent of the Chinese mothers and 68 percent of the Japanese mothers reported reading to their children this often.

American mothers are also more likely to take their young children on outings or excursions than are Chinese and Japanese mothers. We asked mothers how many times in the past month they or their husbands had taken their kindergarteners to places such as movies, museums, sporting events, or the zoo. American parents took their children on outings nearly twice as frequently as the Chinese parents, and nearly seven times as often as the Japanese parents. The low frequency of such outings in Taipei or Sendai does not indicate a dearth of interesting places to visit, but reflects the conviction of Asian parents that young children do not necessarily benefit from such experiences. American parents, by contrast, appear to believe that it is important to introduce young children to the world beyond the home and neighborhood, and the earlier the better. Shopping carts in American supermarkets come with seats for young children, all but the fanciest restaurants are equipped with kiddie seats, and museums and zoos rent strollers—all in an effort to accommodate families on outings with their infants and young children.

Different attitudes about early stimulation are also found in the degree to which parents try to teach academic skills to their preschool and kindergarten children. Nine out of ten American mothers of kindergarteners said they had taught their children the alphabet at home. Fewer than a third of the Chinese and Japanese mothers said they had taught their children the symbols used to denote the sounds of the Chinese and Japanese languages. When mothers were asked about whether they had attempted to teach numbers at home, 90 percent of the American mothers, 64 percent of the Chinese mothers, and 36 percent of the Japanese mothers answered affirmatively.

Asian mothers believe that whatever teaching they do with their preschool children should be as informal as possible. Rather than drilling their children on counting and calculating, they are more likely to incorporate their teaching into an interesting activity. We observed an example of this on a Tokyo subway train. A preschool child, seated with his mother, was peering out the window, trying to read the station signs. Pointing his finger at one sign, he pronounced the sounds "oo" and "eh," but faltered on a third symbol. The mother supplied the third sound, "no," whereupon the little boy looked delighted: "It's Ueno Station!" The mother did not follow up by attempting to drill her son on the third symbol, but allowed him to enjoy the thrill of having read the sign. Her goal seemed to be more to maintain his interest and curiosity than to teach him a particular fact.

Many American parents would seize on this situation as an

opportunity to engage in direct teaching. For example, we recently overheard an interchange between an American father and his first- or second-grader. "What's the name of a dinosaur that begins with A?" asked the father. "Allosaur." "Right! And how about one that begins with B?" the father continued. "Brontosaur." And through the alphabet they went. When the boy faltered, the father supplied the name. Long after the child appeared to lose interest, the father persisted; what had started as a game ended in a tedious lesson.

The views parents hold about the preschool years have direct consequences for the rearing of their children. Chinese and Japanese parents are satisfied if their children develop into outgoing social beings who adapt satisfactorily in a group. They guide their children and assist them, but make few explicit demands beyond learning the routines of everyday living. American parents have different goals. They expect that both they and the preschool will provide the all-around preparation needed for success in elementary school, and they demand a great deal of themselves and of the teachers in providing appropriate experiences to meet these broad goals.

Preschool and Kindergarten

Differences in Asian and American strategies for early socialization at home are evident in the organization of preschools and kindergartens, and in parents' expectations for what these programs should accomplish. Americans distinguish between preschools (or day-care centers) and kindergartens. Chinese and Japanese do not. They combine programs for three-through-five-year-olds in a single administrative unit, reflecting their belief that all these children remain in the age of innocence. American kindergartens are attached to elementary schools and are supervised by elementary school principals, thereby defining the kindergarten as the first rung in the elementary school ladder. Preschool and kindergarten programs in China, Taiwan, and Japan, by contrast, have no physical or administrative relationship to elementary schools.

Japanese and Chinese parents expect their children to learn little more than social skills in nursery school and kindergarten. They enroll their children in these programs primarily to help them learn to enjoy group life and to participate effectively in it. They believe that the opportunities at preschool for free play and group activities are more effective for learning social behavior than those in the home and neighborhood. Asian parents do not expect the preschool to emphasize intellectual or academic advancement, and they are satisfied if their children learn how to be self-sufficient, to follow routines, and to master such practical skills as eating, toileting, dressing, greeting adults, solving conflicts, paying attention, and carrying out instructions. In line with these expectations, here is how one Japanese kindergarten teacher described her goals for her pupils: "I want children to develop a good self-image, to enjoy the companionship of both children and adults, to have a background of childlike experiences. I mean by this, loving care and time to play and pretend—to hear stories, songs, and poetry, to experience a leisurely paced life, and to have opportunities and encouragement to try the daring, creative, and messy."

American parents have very different expectations. They look to early education programs to provide cognitive and academic stimulation for their children. Americans generally agree that three- and four-year-olds need to have opportunities for gaining social competence, but they consider that by the time a child is five years old—the kindergarten year—the main function of the school's program should be to get children ready for elementary school. In addition to personal-social development, "school readiness" is expected to include a good grounding in the fundamentals of reading and mathematics, and efforts are made to develop curiosity, thinking skills, vocabulary, and general knowledge.

The greater emphasis on direct teaching of academic and cognitive skills in American kindergartens was evident in a study we conducted of groups of five-year-olds in Taipei, Sendai, and Minneapolis. In more than three hundred hours of observation in kindergartens, we found that American teachers spent approximately 30 percent of their classroom time in direct efforts to teach academic materials, whereas 20 percent of the Chinese and less than 5 percent of the Japanese classroom time was spent in such efforts. Most of the rest of the time at kindergarten was spent in free play and informal learning, activities that occurred nearly four times as often in Taipei and Sendai classrooms as in Minneapolis.

We also asked mothers how they thought parents could best help their children do well in kindergarten. The two most common answers Japanese mothers gave were to keep the child healthy and to express interest in school activities. Only 2 percent of the Japanese mothers—but nearly half of the American mothers—said they would help their kindergarten children by working with them on educational activities. Chinese mothers fell in between: 29 percent said they would engage in direct educational stimulation.

Achievement in Kindergarten

The American emphasis on cognitive stimulation and direct teaching of academic skills might be expected to result in relatively better test scores for American kindergarten children, and it does. In contrast to the depressing picture of elementary school students presented in Chapter 2, American kindergarteners hold their own, or even outscore their Asian peers, on tests of general knowledge, vocabulary, memory, and ability to carry out instructions. Even in mathematics and reading achievement the differences between American and Asian children were limited. American children did nearly as well in mathematics as the Chinese kindergarteners and better in reading than the Japanese kindergarteners.

Only a year separates the ages of the kindergarteners and the first graders, but during this time the performance of the American children deteriorates relative to that of the Chinese and Japanese children. Dramatic shifts must occur in children's experiences in order for the relative status of the children's achievement to change so strikingly, and, indeed, Chinese, Japanese, and American conceptions of childhood all undergo significant changes at about the time children enter elementary school.

THE AGE OF REASON

The Chinese words most frequently used to denote what we have called the age of innocence translate literally as the "period of not knowing." Entry into the age of reason marks the beginning of the transformation to the state of knowing and also coincides with the time children enter elementary school. The family begins to mobilize itself to provide the kinds of experiences and assistance that will be necessary for the child to become a "knowing" person. Asian parents believe that this transformation is long and difficult, and that teachers alone cannot accomplish it. They believe that they must assume much greater involvement in their children's development and learning if their children are to acquire the skills necessary for functioning effectively in society.

American parents do not make such a clear distinction between periods of not knowing and knowing, but the child's entrance into school is an important cue for changing the parent-child relationship. When their children progress from kindergarten to elementary school, American parents believe the school should take on many of the responsibilities that they had previously assumed themselves. Paradoxically, just as Asian parents are gearing up to invest large amounts of time and energy in supporting their children's academic activities, American parents begin to pull back, satisfied that they have provided a foundation that will enable their children to take advantage of what the school will offer.

Chinese and Japanese children no doubt find it difficult to understand the changes in the family's behavior when they enter first grade. Parents who had been nurturant and permissive become authorities who demand obedience, respect, and adherence to their rules and goals. The freedom and indulgence that were permitted earlier are less likely to be granted, and children are expected to abandon their relatively carefree existence for discipline and devotion to study. Studying and doing well in school become the child's principal responsibilities, and the Asian conception of healthy development tends to involve how well children meet these responsibilities. The transition is less abrupt for Japanese than for Chinese children. Children in both cultures are expected to conform closely to the rules at school, but tolerance in Japanese homes for children's dependent and disruptive behavior is greater than in Chinese families. It is better, suggests the Japanese parent, for the child to display negative aspects of behavior in the privacy of the home than in the group.

Lois Peak describes the Japanese belief in this way: "The home, or *uchi,* is the private, intimate arena in which one can relax, let all of one's feelings show, and expect indulgence from other members of the family. Within the *uchi* a healthy amount of self-indulgence, regressive behavior, and mild aggression are not only cheerfully tolerated but also encouraged as an indication of intimacy and trust."[1] Contrasted with the *uchi* is the outside world, where harmony and sensitivity to the needs of the group become dominant goals. The freedom and expressiveness possible within the family are believed to ease the adaptation to life outside the home.

American children experience a very different type of transition from kindergarten to elementary school. Their entry into elementary school is not accompanied by strong parental demands for academic excellence or devotion to homework, and demands do not increase much during the succeeding years of elementary school. Schoolwork is considered to be the responsibility of teachers and students, rather than a major concern for parents. On the other hand, American parents expect their children to be successful in other ways, including social acceptance, appearance, prowess in sports, and thinking skills.

Parental Involvement

The greater tendency of Asian than American parents to share responsibility for their children's progress in school is evident in the amount of time American parents spend assisting their children with schoolwork. According to the mothers we interviewed, American children received less help each week at home than did children in Sendai or Taipei—partly because the American children were assigned less homework. In Chinese families, this duty is distributed nearly equally among the mother, father, and siblings. In Japan, the father leaves for work early in the morning, returns home late at night, works most Saturdays, and has only Sunday to spend with the family. As a result, Japanese fathers are seldom available to interact with their children, and the mothers must assume the primary responsibility for child-rearing.

Because so many of the Japanese mother's duties revolve around schoolwork and because she is intensely devoted to her task, she has become known as the education mom. Westerners frequently misinterpret what this title implies, and it is important to clarify what the *kyoiku mama* perceives as her duty to her child. In contrast to the common stereotype, the Japanese mother does not hover over her child, urging him to study or attempting to teach academic skills. She does not adopt the role of a pushy, demanding, home-bound tutor.

It is more accurate to describe the Japanese mother as a provider of a nurturant and protected atmosphere for learning. She is ready to assist her child in doing homework if she can, but her main goals are to promote her child's interest and involvement in school and to make sure that he is progressing appropriately. As much as possible, she shifts responsibility for doing homework to the child. For example, when asked who was responsible for seeing that the child's homework was completed, Japanese mothers were much more likely than either Chinese or American mothers to say that it was the child's responsibility.

Many critics have attempted to attribute the low involvement of American parents to the tendency for mothers to work outside the home and to the breakdown of the nuclear family. Our data suggest that these are not major factors. The percentage of mothers employed full time in Minneapolis, Sendai, and Taipei did not differ appreciably (35 percent, 30 percent, and 33 percent, respectively). And in Beijing, 97 percent of mothers were employed full time. So maternal employment clearly does not offer a satisfactory explanation for the lower degree of American parents' involvement in their children's academic work. Nor does the incidence of single-parent families. Eighty-one percent of the families in our Minneapolis sample, for example, were intact. American parents' low level of involvement in their young children's schooling cannot be explained easily by demographics. Instead, we believe that it reflects American assumptions about the role that parents should play.

School and Home

Japanese and Chinese appear to maintain a relatively sharp differentiation between the functions of school and home. Schools are primarily held responsible for developing academic skills, and the social skills required for integration into group life; the home is responsible for supporting the school's role and for providing a healthy emotional environment for the child. Parents and teachers work together, but do not duplicate one another's roles.

Americans, by contrast, seem to expect that schools will take on responsibility for many more aspects of the child's life. They have turned over to the school many of the functions that traditionally have been performed by families: education about sex, drugs, minority relations, illnesses, nutrition, fire prevention, and many other topics. Each time a new need arises—whether it is how to behave in an earthquake or how to avoid dental plaque—Americans assume that the schools rather than the parents will respond to their children's need for information. In addition to setting aside special times for such instruction, schools are expected to help the children establish good peer relations, to provide counseling when children encounter problems, and to provide the general support and assistance necessary for sound emotional development.

The close cooperation in Asian cultures between parents and teachers leads to a strong emphasis on communication between home and school, reflected in a simple but very effective technique employed in both Japanese and Chinese schools. Each child carries a small notebook back and forth between home and school. A parent must indicate in the notebook that the child has completed the daily homework assignment and may write about any general problems or difficulties of which the teacher should be aware. In turn, teachers use the notebooks to communicate with parents about homework assignments, test results, special activities in school, and the child's behavior. Parents and teachers are expected to check the notebook every day.

Only through this degree of intimate knowledge of what is happening at school can parents hope to be aware of the ways they can help their children and provide a home environment conducive to studying. Parent-teacher conferences, parental visits to the school, and meetings of parent-teacher associations in America do not provide the kind of day-to-day feedback that parents get through the notebooks carried back and forth by Chinese and Japanese children. If a parent seeks to monitor his child's performance closely, he needs such information. But as we have seen, American parents do not envision for themselves the role of monitor.

Not surprisingly, one of the most frequent complaints of American teachers is that they do not get adequate support from the home. Just when the demands of school increase and support at home is most needed, parents pull back, diminishing their own role in their child's development.

TECHNIQUES OF SOCIALIZATION

The techniques societies use for socializing children are as interesting as the differences in the societies' conceptions of childhood. The distinction among societies is not in whether their members use particular techniques—for many techniques are used by all societies to some degree—but in how pervasively and purposefully they are applied. Several techniques appear to be more widely and consciously applied in Asian than in American societies: the use of models, the use of groups as agents of social control, and the use of explicit methods for teaching routines.

Modeling

Modeling is commonly used to shape human behavior. The idea is straightforward: Find people who exemplify the ideals held by the society and select aspects of their lives that can be described simply and dramatically. Keep the descriptions about each person consistent, and repeat the descriptions frequently, so that the characteristics of the models become widely known. The models of course are much more complex human beings than they appear in the stories about them, but it is not the complexity of their lives that is important. They are selected because the culture values the characteristics that they are reputed to display and encourages young children to imitate them. And older children and adults are expected to understand the principles demonstrated in the models' behavior.

The United States has had many well-known models. Earlier in this century every American schoolchild was aware of the frugality and inventiveness of Franklin, the compassion of Nightingale, the creativity of Edison, Steinmetz, and Curie. Children could articulate what Honest Abe stood for, and why it was important to be like Washington, who could not tell a lie. The accomplishments and behavior of these people were held before children as examples of what they should admire and strive to emulate.

For the most part, such cultural models have been displaced in the United States today. Children no longer talk about the young Lincoln studying by the fireplace, or about the long hours of work that led to Marie Curie's discoveries about radioactivity. America is particularly devoid of any models who are children. Adventurous astronauts served as models for some American children and youths, but in recent years American children's models have tended to be not heroes of service, science, or government, but sports figures and entertainers. No conscious national efforts are made to designate these people as models, except perhaps by sportswriters or film publicists. Rather, the new models emerge because of their hairstyles, dance techniques, material possessions, manner of dress, or athletic talents. Only in American minority groups have specific efforts been made in recent years to introduce models for children. Martin Luther King, Jr., and Sojourner Truth are held up as exemplifying bravery and dedication. Otherwise, our era is particularly barren of the kinds of models that were formerly popular. Indeed, there appears to have been a deliberate effort to expose models' feet of clay—for example, Jefferson's slaveholding and the rapacity of captains of industry.

The situation is very different in Asia. Every schoolchild in Japan nods knowingly when the name of Ninomiya Kinjiro is mentioned. This youth, who lived in the Edo period nearly two hundred years ago, was diligent in his efforts to learn. He was never without his books, and he used every possible moment to study, even while he was helping his mother around the house or gathering firewood in the forest. Statues of Kinjiro, with firewood on his back and a book in front of him, may still be found in schoolyards throughout Japan. Recalling Kinjiro's efforts, teachers and parents ask how students today, with so few obstacles and such splendid opportunities, can have any valid reason for shirking their studies.

Perhaps the most pervasive use of models is in China, where

there have been long-time efforts to develop models. Currently popular, for example, are the two young Lan women, Panxing and Yang, bank employees who bravely resisted bank robbers, despite being cruelly beaten. Yang died, but Panxing crawled out of the bank and informed the police, who eventually captured the robbers. Lai Ning is another recent model. Stories extol the bravery of this young primary school boy, who died in his efforts to put out a budding forest fire. But by far the most popular model throughout China during the last half century has been Lei Feng, known as Chairman Mao's good soldier. This young man was killed during the Korean War, but his dedication and kindness before his death have made him a model for all citizens. Since the early 1960s, Chinese children have been exhorted to learn from Lei Feng.

Lei Feng modeled himself after the local Communist Party secretary, and from adolescence he displayed positive forms of behavior, such as washing and mending his fellow soldiers' clothes, giving his lunch to a comrade who forgot his lunch, and buying pencils and a notebook to help another soldier study. He instructed young people to be good citizens and to heed Chairman Mao's calls to "Study hard and make progress every day" and to "Serve the people." Children's books about Lei Feng not only describe how he modeled his behavior after that of the Party secretary and Chairman Mao, but also show how others who adopted Lei Feng as a model ultimately became models themselves. Children are thus confronted with tier upon tier of models, all studying hard and working diligently and selflessly for important causes.

Chinese children encounter these models in books, magazines, television programs, and the pages of their elementary school readers. Charles Ridley and his colleagues analyzed the themes in these readers in order to determine the values that were expounded.[2] The most popular theme was social and personal responsibility, as exemplified by devotion to duty, obedience and deference, thrift and frugality, prudence, honesty, and neatness and order. The second most common theme was achievement. Stories dealing with this theme were concerned with how individuals achieve through diligence and persistence, or through cleverness. Like McGuffey's readers in the nineteenth century, the textbooks teach reading and inculcate social values at the same time.

Virtuous themes are not specific to mainland China; they are also prevalent in readers used by elementary school children in Taiwan. Sun Yat-sen and Chiang Kai-shek substitute for Mao Zedong and Deng Xiaoping, but their message is much the same. For example, in describing the content of one of the stories in his reader, a fifth-grade Taiwan student concluded, "Dr. Sun Yat-sen said we should do things for others. Therefore, we should be like that"—much the same message as Mao's "Serve the people."

Although Americans make little effort to present models for American children, modeling happens anyway, of course. Styles or fads are clear examples. But a nation that is falling behind in its efforts to educate its children has reason to consider whether a process that can change the hairstyle of a vast majority of students might not be effective in motivating students to devote more attention to their studies. Men and women who pursue the acquisition of knowledge should be as worthy of emulation as sports heroes and rock stars, and their stories should be as compelling. Developing models, however, requires a conscious effort. Bart Simpson, the popular television "underachiever," reveals our national values: Americans view "nerds" and "bookworms" as models to be avoided, but have no positive models for students to imitate.

Group Control

Americans are proud of their individualism; Asians are proud of their group orientation. We in the West emphasize the importance of the individual and the development of an independent, self-directed, self-motivated child. Raising an independent child is not a central concern for Chinese and Japanese parents; much more importance is given instead to establishing interdependent relations between the child and other members of the family and society.

The concerns of teachers reflect these values. When teachers are asked what behavior exhibited by a preschool child would worry them most, American teachers cite aggressive behavior. In Japan, the child who plays alone arouses the most concern. Japanese teachers point out that the aggressive child at least is socially engaged, and with proper guidance can learn more acceptable ways of social interaction. The isolated child is more difficult to socialize, for by being alone he has little opportunity to practice social skills. American teachers, in contrast, consider playing alone to be a positive sign, an indication of independence.[3]

The individual in Asia is typically defined through participation in groups—family, school, community, company, and nation. Primary obligations are to the group, and competition is between groups, not between individuals within groups. Individuals are aware of differences in the relative status of members of the group, but Asians minimize the significance of these differences in order to increase group cohesiveness.

Identification with a group builds a strong common bond among its members, and Chinese and Japanese societies make vigorous efforts to foster it. In Japanese preschools, for example, children at different age levels wear hats and smocks of different colors; in Japanese elementary schools the students in a particular grade may be distinguished by the color of the stripes and laces of their tennis shoes. In China, children become members of the Young Pioneers after their entry into elementary school. At a formal ceremony they receive the red Young Pioneer scarves that they will then wear to school every day.

Group identification provides a strong, effective means of heightening children's motivation toward particular goals. Children may shrug off teachers' efforts to exert control, but they find it harder to disregard the opinions and evaluations of peers. Moreover, if the accomplishments of one's classroom or subgroup are prized over those of any individual, the performance of all children becomes the responsibility of each member of the group. So children quickly realize how important it is for all members to participate effectively in the group's activities and to regard their responsibility to the group as more important than their own advancement. This does not mean that individual accomplishment is disparaged; rather, it becomes something that enhances the prestige of the child's group and family.

As a result of group participation, cooperation comes easily for most Asian children—something we observed while watching a well-known American psychologist demonstrate a problem-solving task in a Chinese second-grade classroom. She gave each of three children a short stick and showed them a small container with a narrow opening. She placed a ball in the container and told them their task was to remove the ball, using only the sticks. Success is easily attained through cooperation, but otherwise is very unlikely. The three Chinese children quickly settled into a cooperative approach; by working together, they rapidly solved a problem that appears to be simple but has often challenged the more individualistically oriented young children in the West.

The power of the group is also used as a means of motivating children. Parents remind an indolent child that failure to do well in school will bring shame on the family. The child is made aware that his poor grades can cause his family to lose face, not merely because he failed to study hard, but because his family would be regarded as not fulfilling its duties toward him.

American families also use shame as a technique, but in a very different fashion. Rather than reminding a child that poor performance may bring shame to her family, an American parent is more likely to tell her, "You should be ashamed of yourself for getting grades like that!" A child may find it tolerable to allow self-approval to lag at times; it is much more difficult to face the consequences of bringing shame to a whole family or social group.

Teaching techniques practiced in Asian classrooms also reflect the importance placed on group influence. Asian elementary school teachers aspire to be well-informed guides, explaining details when necessary, but more typically asking children to generate their own solutions and calling on other children to evaluate the accuracy or relevance of the answers. They spend little of their time lecturing. In such a group-oriented situation, the child who has not studied and is unable to respond with a sensible answer faces potential derision by the group—a factor far more difficult to disregard than the scorn of the teacher alone.

American classrooms look quite different. American teachers are more likely than Asian teachers to lecture to children and to assume personal responsibility for judging what is correct and what is not. Generally, we have found that American teachers and other adults are more reluctant than Asians to transfer responsibility from themselves to children. By failing to do so, they lose one of the most powerful sources of motivation available for children: peer acceptance or disapproval.

Explicit Teaching of Routines

A third technique for socialization that is much more fully exploited in Asia than in the United States is the explicit teaching of routines—instruction in the seemingly minor details of behavior that often are left to chance in our own culture. Teachers take time, early in the first grade, to teach children how to organize their desks, use the bathroom, change their clothes for different activities, and collect the necessary articles for their pencil boxes. In later years children are taught how to answer questions loudly and clearly, take notes, and organize their written answers so that the steps leading to the solution are readily discernible. Rather than expecting children to be able to demonstrate a particular form of behavior spontaneously or in response to requests or commands, Asian teachers explicitly teach the component skills that are necessary for the smooth operation of classroom routines. Thus, the efficiency of Asian classrooms is not attributable to more

91

rapid motor or cognitive development of Asian children, but to the fact that children are formally taught, gradually and step by step, a repertoire of routines that can form the basis of instruction in academic subjects.

American teachers seldom directly teach classroom routines. They believe it is more important to spend the available time teaching the substance of reading, mathematics, and social studies, forgetting that mastery of classroom routines may be critical in order for the teaching of higher-order skills to be effective. Even as early as elementary school, children can benefit from knowing how to underline, outline, organize, and summarize the content of a lesson—study skills that some American university students have failed to learn. These are not skills that most people develop spontaneously, but, as a visit to a fourth- or fifth-grade Chinese or Japanese classroom will reveal, they are skills that elementary school children can be taught.

Foreign visitors are often dazzled by the performance of young children in Asia. Concerts by three-year-old Japanese violinists and demonstrations of martial arts by eight-year-old Chinese children frequently become the topics of stories that foreign visitors tell to their friends when they return home. The children perform well because they have mastered the components of each of these complex acts. When young American children are taught in a similar fashion, they, too, are able to charm audiences with their skill and proficiency. Yet Americans resist teaching children in this way, especially in academic matters.

The resistance stems from criticism that explicit teaching of component skills produces automatons rather than creative children. But there is little validity to this argument. Creativity in a domain depends on mastery of basic skills; it is not inhibited by their mastery. No American adult will argue that his skill in tennis or golf came without attention to details, or that the opportunities for expressiveness that were opened up through the use of a computer would have been possible if he had not learned such elementary skills as moving the cursor, saving files, and following the routines of a word processing program. Yet we uphold in our culture a false dichotomy between knowledge and skill on one hand, and creativity on the other.

DEFINING THE PROBLEM

Most parents, American as well as Asian, acknowledge that families strongly influence their children's academic success. Even so, American families generally appear to be less successful than Asian families in exerting a positive influence. The problem might simply be the cultural differences in the goals parents have for their children. As we have seen, Asian parents regard doing well in school as the single most important task facing their children. American parents seek to balance academic achievement with other goals, such as developing smooth social skills, high self-esteem, and broad extracurricular interests. Striving for academic excellence, therefore, may be weaker among American children because of the conflicting priorities held by their parents and the resulting deemphasis of academic achievement.

This is only one way to define the problem. Many American parents simply don't know how to help their children become high achievers. The problem is not merely that they fail to emphasize academic achievement, but that they operate on the basis of inappropriate assumptions about when they should intervene, about how they should balance the relative influences of home and school, and about what the most effective socialization techniques are.

American families also overlook techniques that are particularly effective with young children: the use of models whose attributes children can emulate, the involvement of the peer group as a powerful source of motivation, and the adoption of routines that provide a foundation for later learning. These techniques for increasing children's motivation for academic achievement are available; we wonder why Americans are ambivalent about using them.

Chapter 5

Effort and Ability

Americans consider education to be both a basic entitlement and an obligation of all citizens. Through education, people not only better themselves, but also acquire the knowledge necessary for responsible participation in a free economy and a democratic government. This emphasis on the importance of education to the individual and to society is one of the most frequently voiced aspects of America's national image. Nevertheless, we are persuaded that it is at odds with a less frequently discussed but conflicting American belief that innate differences in intellectual ability limit what can be expected from large numbers of the country's citizens. In education, this tenet is translated to mean that many American children are incapable of mastering the basic academic curriculum of their schools. As we will see, this assumption has had a destructive effect on our educational system.

Americans like to view themselves as rugged individualists who can accomplish whatever goals they set if they work hard enough. But somehow this belief seems to have been eroded. We and others[1] have found that American children, teachers, and parents emphasize innate abilities as a component of success more strongly than their Chinese and Japanese counterparts do. All three societies acknowledge that accomplishment cannot occur without work, but they differ in their beliefs about what people can achieve by work alone.

An overemphasis on innate abilities has insidious implications for children's development and education. Children who believe that their high ability is sufficient to ensure success find little reason to work hard. Alternatively, children who perceive themselves as having low ability and doubt that they can master their lessons through continued effort also have little reason to work hard. Many American students apparently hold the latter belief. In contrast, Asian students, confident that the time they invest will lead to mastery of the academic curriculum, work long hours at their studies. Chinese and Japanese societies allow no excuses for lack of progress in school; regardless of one's current level of performance, opportunities for advancement are always believed to be available through more effort. High scores on a test are interpreted as a sign of diligence. Low scores are not regarded as a sign of stupidity, but simply as an indication that the student has not yet learned what will ultimately be possible through persistence and hard work.

Beliefs about effort, ability, and achievement in Chinese, Japanese, and American societies have far-reaching consequences for learning and for the organization of education. An emphasis on innate ability makes Americans preoccupied with categorizing children as a basis for deciding who can benefit from particular kinds of education. Expectations for "low ability" children are reduced, and they finish their education with inadequate skills and insufficient knowledge for finding jobs and adapting successfully to contemporary society. We suggest that the American emphasis on innate abilities is harmful and is undermining the pursuit of public education—indeed, of democracy itself.

THE AMERICAN EMPHASIS ON ABILITY

Children born into a particular society gradually acquire the beliefs, values, and attitudes held by its members, and use them to explain and interpret their world. To understand why American parents and children invoke ability so frequently in explaining behavior, we must look at the history of this concept in American society.

The American interest in innate ability has been evident for many decades. Early in this century, Americans greeted the intelligence-testing movement with great enthusiasm. Alfred Binet, the French psychologist who created the first intelligence test, intended it to be a simple, reliable means of identifying children who would not benefit from traditional schooling. His test was effective for this purpose, and through various improvements and adaptations it became a valuable tool for clinicians dealing with children. But American psychologists, such as Lewis Terman, who popularized the test in the United States, placed far greater importance on it as a measure of innate abilities than Binet had intended.[2]

It is unclear whether the testing movement intensified Americans' beliefs in innate ability or was merely a consequence of existing beliefs. One thing is certain: The notion that intelligence could be measured was widely lauded by educators, and its consequences for education were rapidly spelled out. This excerpt from an address to the 1920 meeting of the American Psychological Association is typical:

> What we have learned about the influence of environment on mental traits and the failure of environment to alter them materially; what we are now learning about the constancy of the intelligence quotients, and the fact that mental alertness is given like retentiveness once for all with one's native constitution, magnifies the function of the school in selecting individuals and minimizes its function in training them.[3]

Such pronouncements had a widespread influence. Armed with "scientific" tests, educators could quantify individual differences in intelligence and use them to determine a child's likelihood of future success. Teachers could presumably spare dull children the pain of confronting tasks that they would never be expected to master and supplement the curriculum of bright children so their abilities could be realized more fully.

In contrast, Asian societies greeted the intelligence testing movement with less enthusiasm. Although there were Chinese and Japanese translations of the Binet tests, their use was far more restricted than in the United States. The notion of innate, fixed abilities rarely entered debates over educational policy in either Japan or China.

THE ASIAN EMPHASIS ON EFFORT

In Asia, the emphasis on effort and the relative disregard for innate abilities are derived from Confucian philosophy. Confucius was interested above all in the moral perfectibility of mankind. He rejected categorization of human beings as good or bad, and stressed the potential for improving moral conduct through the creation of favorable environmental conditions. His view was gradually extended to all aspects of human behavior. Human beings were considered to be malleable, and like clay, subject to molding by the events of everyday life. Differences among individuals in innate abilities were recognized, for no one can claim that all people are born with the same endowments. But more important was the degree to which a person was willing to maximize these abilities through hard work.

A typical example of the Confucian position is found in the writings of the Chinese philosopher Hsun Tzu, who wrote, "Achievement consists of never giving up. . . . If there is no dark and dogged will, there will be no shining accomplishment; if there is no dull and determined effort, there will be no brilliant achievement."[4] Lack of achievement, therefore, is attributed to insufficient effort rather than to a lack of ability or to personal or environmental obstacles.

People in Asia recount the basic precepts of this view in many vivid folk stories and sayings. For example, the famous story of Li Po, a poet who lived over a thousand years ago, is still told in Chinese elementary school readers.[5] The story is as follows: Li was walking by a small stream and saw a white-haired old woman sitting beside a rock grinding a piece of iron. Perplexed, he asked her what she was doing. "Making a needle," she replied. This answer was even more perplexing, and Li Po asked her how a piece of iron could be ground into a needle. "All you need is perseverance," said the old woman. "If you have a strong will and do not fear hardship, a piece of iron can be ground into a needle." Li Po thought about her answer and became ashamed. He realized that someone like himself would never make progress if he failed to study hard, and from then on he was a diligent student.

Equally famous stories include one about a man who showed his disbelieving townsfolk that it was possible to move a mountain if one persisted year after year on the project. Many short sayings and mottoes also portray the productive consequences of planning and hard work, such as "The slow bird must start out early" and "The rock can be transformed into a gem only through daily polishing."

The belief in the ultimate positive effects of hard work is not an abstract credo, but a practical guide in the everyday lives of most contemporary Chinese and Japanese. Japanese schoolchildren are able to tell you, *"Yareba dekiru"* (If you try hard you can do it), or that they really seek to be a *"gambaru kodomo"* (a child who strives his or her hardest). Adults, too, are guided by such phrases. Recently, for example, one of our students recounted a story about her father, a successful Japanese physician. As a student, he had barely made the cut-off point for admission to medical school. Chastened by this near catastrophe, he vowed to work as hard as possible, and through great effort graduated at the very top of his class. Prominently displayed on the wall of his office is the Japanese saying *"Doryoku ni masaru, tensai nashi"* (Even genius cannot transcend effort).

BELIEFS OF CHILDREN, MOTHERS, AND TEACHERS

Philosophical and anecdotal evidence may be interesting, but it is not always persuasive. Can we actually demonstrate differences in the relative emphasis given to ability and effort by large numbers of Chinese, Japanese, and Americans?

We asked fifth-graders in Sendai, Taipei, and Minneapolis to rate the degree to which they agreed or disagreed with the following statement: "The tests you take can show how much or how little natural ability you have." The children's responses are displayed in Figure 5.1. Students in Sendai and Taipei were more likely to disagree than were students in Minneapolis. That is, Chinese and Japanese children were less likely than American children to accept the proposal that tests can reveal natural ability.

We tapped mothers' beliefs by suggesting that among the factors influencing children's performance were effort, ability, difficulty of the task, and luck. We asked the mothers which they thought was most important, next most important, and so on. After obtaining their rank ordering, we asked them to distribute ten points among the four factors according to the importance each has for a child's schoolwork. The way mothers in each culture assigned their points is shown in Figure 5.2. All three groups of mothers gave the greatest number of points to effort, but Asian mothers gave more points to effort than did the American mothers. When it came to assigning points to ability, American mothers assigned significantly more points than did the Chinese and Japanese mothers.

Using another approach, we asked children in Beijing and Chicago to rate the importance of effort and innate ability in influencing children's performance in school. Ratings of the influence of effort were very similar, as can be seen in Figure 5.3, but

FIGURE 5.1
Children's degree of agreement with the statement "The tests you
take can show how much or how little natural ability you have."
(Scale: 7 = Strongly Agree; 1 = Strongly Disagree)

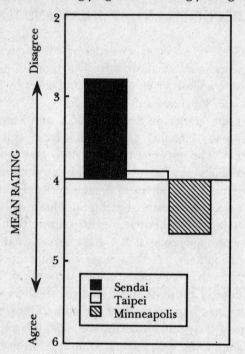

American children rated the influence of innate ability higher
than did the Chinese.

Here is a final example. We asked mothers of elementary school
children in Minneapolis and Taipei how early in a child's life they
thought it was possible to predict scores on achievement tests that
would be given at the end of high school. We reasoned that
mothers who believed in the importance and stability of innate
abilities would give earlier estimates than mothers who deempha-
sized innate abilities; that is, that American mothers would give

FIGURE 5.2

Number of points (out of ten) that mothers assigned to indicate relative importance of factors that affect academic achievement.

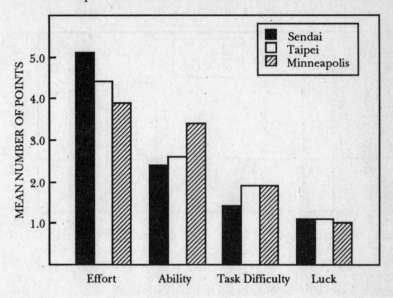

earlier ages than Asian mothers. In fact, they did. For example, 38 percent of Minneapolis mothers, but only 10 percent of Chinese mothers, believed that it was possible to make such predictions before the end of elementary school.

No matter how we asked the questions or to whom we directed them, the answers were consistent: Americans were more likely to assign greater importance to innate ability than were Chinese and Japanese.

FIGURE 5.3

Children's evaluation of the importance of effort and ability
for success in school.

(Scale: 5 = Very Important; 1 = Not at All Important)

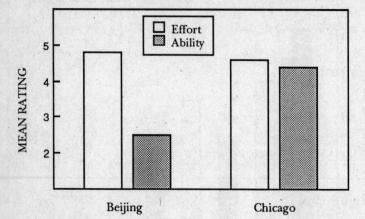

CULTURAL MODELS OF LEARNING

The relative emphasis given to ability and to effort has direct implications for the way people think about learning. In American society, learning tends to be regarded as an all-or-none process. A student who is "bright" is expected just to "get it," whereas duller students are assumed to lack the requisite ability for ever learning certain material. Under an "ability" model, motivation to try hard depends to a great extent on the individual child's assessment of whether he has the ability to succeed. By contrast, an "effort" model, such as the Chinese and Japanese tend to hold, portrays learning as gradual and incremental, something that almost by definition must be acquired over a long time. Progress is analogous to a ranking in tennis or squash. No matter what your level, there is someone at the next higher level whom you can challenge with a chance of winning. Progress is attained step by step and is potentially available to anyone.

If one subscribes to the effort model, errors are seen as a natural part of the learning process. Under the ability model, in contrast, errors may be interpreted as an indication of failure, and may imply that the potential to learn is lacking. In American classrooms, teachers go to great lengths to prevent failure. Rather than have children risk failing a task that may be difficult, teachers tend to give easier tasks to students they judge to be of lower ability. In one study, researchers tracked reading assignments of first-grade children in high and low reading groups. Those in the high groups were given an average of 1100 words to read each week; those in low groups, only 400.[6] Under such circumstances, how could there fail to be great differences in learning between the high and low groups? Chinese and Japanese teachers do not adjust the curriculum according to children's ease of learning, but emphasize instead that slower students may need to put out extra effort in order to keep up with the curriculum.

Differing models of learning are also revealed in the ways that grades are interpreted in Asian and American cultures. In Chinese and Japanese classrooms, grades on tests are public knowledge. In a fifth-grade Taipei classroom we visited, the class was doing mental arithmetic, an exercise in which the teacher held up cards containing computation problems. The children solved the problems in their heads and wrote down their answers. When all of the problems had been presented, the children exchanged papers and corrected each other's answers. After the papers were returned to their owners, the teacher asked, "How many of you missed one problem? Two? Three?" Children continued to raise their hands in response as the teacher proceeded: "Eighteen?" "Nineteen?" There was little hesitation or embarrassment apparent in the children's reactions.

In the typical American classroom, such a procedure would have become increasingly threatening as the number of errors mounted. Grades are considered a private affair in American classrooms. Because a low score may be interpreted to mean that a child is "dumb" and lacks ability, disclosure of low grades is potentially embarrassing. So when American teachers hand back test papers, they often fold them carefully so that the grade is visible only to the student to whom the paper belongs. In the Asian classroom, a large number of errors is likely to be regarded as indicating that a student is fatigued or has failed to study. Rather than revealing a low potential, errors represent an opportunity to learn much more if the student were to try hard in the future.

Our argument is not that Americans subscribe only to an ability-based model of learning, but that they apply the model in many more situations than do Chinese and Japanese. Americans do understand the effort-based model of learning and frequently apply it in domains such as dance and music. The dance teacher does not assume that students will be able to express themselves in movement solely through some natural proficiency, but knows that they must gradually be taught the skills that will make expressiveness possible. The rudiments of dance are taught slowly over a period of years. The less skilled dancer is thought of as being at an earlier stage in the progression toward higher and higher skill.

More often, however, Americans talk of ability even when they recognize the importance of effort. A husky American boy may be ready to spend long hours practicing football, but his slender high school classmate, who possibly could become an outstanding quarterback, may not be willing to venture as far as the locker room, out of the belief that he lacks the necessary physique and coordination. If he were less influenced by his assumptions about natural endowments, he might expend the effort that would enable him to join his classmate on the team.

We see a similar phenomenon in the way Americans teach art to children. Proficiency in art is widely viewed as dependent on innate talent, and many Americans explain their failure to draw a credible representation of an object as due to a lack of ability: "I am just no good at drawing." This explanation would be unacceptable to a Chinese or Japanese. "Oh, no," she might reply. "It is too bad that no one taught you to draw."

The Asian disregard for the limitations posed by an ability model offers children a more optimistic view of the possible outcomes of their efforts than does the model held by most Americans. Through step-by-step training, Asian elementary school children gain a level of skill and confidence that typically exceeds American children's. The slower or even the average American child is not given the explicit instruction and attention that is likely to be concentrated on those who have greater "natural talent and ability."

Beliefs about Mathematics Learning

From our studies and from the observations of other researchers, it seems clear that beliefs about mathematics learning differ in Asian and American societies. American children view learning mathematics as a process of rapid insight rather than lengthy struggle. According to one American researcher in mathematics education, American children appear to believe that if a mathematics problem is solvable, it can be solved in less than ten minutes.[7] The unfortunate result is that American students are likely to give up before they reach genuine understanding.

The fact that Japanese children do not share this belief in the need for ready solutions is illustrated by the experience we had in trying to measure persistence. We wanted to find out whether Asian students would in fact persevere longer than American students when given difficult problems. We planned to give children a mathematics problem that was impossible to solve, and see how long they would spend working on it before they gave up. Although the idea seemed reasonable, our Japanese colleagues convinced us to drop the task after they tried it out with several children. The difficulty? Japanese children, refusing to give up, kept working on the problem long beyond the time our colleagues felt they could justifiably allow the children to keep on trying.

Evidence was found in the computation test described in Chapter 2 that American children do give up faster than Asian children when faced with a difficult problem. Children were asked to solve as many problems as possible within a time limit of twenty minutes. Japanese children attempted the fewest problems and American children attempted the most. Of those problems that were attempted, however, the highest percentage of correct answers at first grade was in Japan (85 percent), the next in Taiwan (75 percent) and the lowest was in Chicago (61 percent). In fifth grade, the pattern was similar: Both Chinese and Japanese students solved about 77 percent of the problems they attempted; American students solved only 51 percent. Needless to say, the American children's strategy of skipping rapidly across the problems did not pay off; they solved a smaller percentage of the problems they attempted, and their overall number of correct answers was also significantly below that of the Asian children.

In sum, the relative importance people assign to factors beyond their control, like ability, compared to factors that they can control, like effort, can strongly influence the way they approach learning. Ability models subvert learning through the effects they have on the goals that parents and teachers set for children and on children's motivation to work hard to achieve these goals. Effort models offer a more hopeful alternative by providing a simple but constructive formula for ensuring gradual change and improvement: Work hard and persist.

EDUCATION AND CATEGORIZATION

Another alarming aspect of an ability model is the effect it has on the organization of our educational system. The seemingly logical and humane consequence of an emphasis on innate differences is that children with different abilities should be educated differently if their full potential is to be realized. Great care is given to assigning children to different groups within a classroom or to different academic tracks, each with its own textbook and curriculum.

A tendency to categorize children has pervaded the American educational system for a long time. It is apparent in the recent explosion of special education classes, but it was evident before that, during the spread of universal education in the United States.

Historical Context

Since the end of the last century, educators concerned with academic standards have aligned themselves with one of two basic positions. The first, which the historian Richard Hofstadter terms "Intellectualism,"[8] holds that when levels of achievement are lower than desired or expected, higher academic standards should be applied to all students. Contemporary adherents of this view define the goal of education as the mastery of core academic subjects by everyone, and they argue that America is suffering an educational crisis because the country has lost sight of this basic goal.

The opposing position regards the intellectualist agenda as old-fashioned—applicable, perhaps, to a time in which education was the prerogative of the elite, but unrealistic in a democratic society in which children of widely different abilities, backgrounds, and interests are to be educated. Those espousing an anti-intellectualist position have argued that the goal of education is to meet the needs of individual students, which may or may not include a primary emphasis on academic learning. The anti-intellectualist position has gradually dominated the debate, and it remains popular today.

The demise and ascendance of these two opposing views has an interesting history. We can trace it through a series of reports issued by the National Education Association (NEA). The first report, issued in 1893, at a time when the school curriculum was still highly academic in content, proposed that "every subject which is taught at all in a secondary school should be taught in the same way and to the same extent to every pupil so long as he pursues it, no matter what the probable destination of the pupil may be or at what point his education is to cease."[9]

107

By 1918, when a second NEA report was released, the function of schools was not stated to be imparting academic learning, but more broadly to "prepare children to be participating citizens in a democratic society."[10] To meet this obligation, schools were expected to respond differentially to the needs of different children, and, the report continued, "The basis of differentiation should be, in the broad sense of the term, vocational." And then, recognizing that some students could benefit from an academically oriented curriculum, it added: "Provision should be made also for those having distinctively academic interests and needs."[11]

These changing currents in educational thinking profoundly affected the school curriculum. Between 1910 and 1950, the proportion of academic subjects in American high school curricula fell by almost 60 percent, while the number of different courses increased tenfold.[12] The old academic curriculum was virtually replaced by the so-called life-adjustment curriculum: an array of courses created to meet what educators perceived to be the range of needs and abilities in a diverse and rapidly increasing population.

Altruistic advocates of the new curriculum contended that such an approach was somehow more democratic, more fair than the old academic curriculum. If all children would study in tracks where they could succeed, then each would have the opportunity to enter society with a positive self-image and with skills that could lead to jobs. But as Richard Hofstadter points out, it was a

> peculiar self-defeating version of "democracy" entertained by these educators [that] somehow made it possible for them to assert that immature, insecure, nervous, retarded slow learners from poor cultural environments were "in no sense inferior" to more mature, secure, confident, gifted children from better cultural environments. This verbal genuflection before "democracy" seems to have enabled them to conceal from themselves that they were, with breathtaking certainty, writing off the majority of the nation's children as being more or less uneducable.[13]

Tracking persists in this country, even at the elementary grades, bolstered by arguments that education is most effective when it is tailored to the particular needs, interests, and abilities of the children. But these arguments ignore the fact that children know that the Robins really are better readers than the Bluebirds, and that their age mates are sorted into classes for "dummies" and classes for smart kids. Such knowledge may enhance the self-image and pride of children who happen to be Robins, but Bluebirds may be stigmatized from their early months in school. Once categorized as slow learners, a vicious cycle begins: They are placed in slower tracks; teachers hold lower expectations for their possible accomplishments, and thus expose them to lower levels of material than they do the more able students; the students come to believe that they indeed are incapable of higher levels of achievement; and many end up dropping out of school.

The educational systems of Japan, Taiwan, and China were relatively unaffected by the changes in educational philosophy fermenting in the United States during this time. Even though American educators advised the Japanese in their reform of education following World War II, Japanese educators, and other Asian educators as well, proceeded to develop educational systems in which students had to adapt to the unwavering standards of excellence of demanding academic curricula.[14] As a result, all children attended the same classes, and whenever groups were formed in a classroom, all levels of skill were represented in each group. Rapid learners practiced their new skills by helping their slower peers, and the motivation of slower learners was strengthened by the enthusiastic encouragement of other members of the class. The net effect was that although individual differences among members of the class remained, the overall level of performance of the class was raised.

The Case of Learning Disabilities

Categorization of children is perhaps most evident in the special education movement, especially as it is concerned with learning disabilities. The diagnosis of learning disabilities has never been purely scientific and objective, and it is influenced as much by cultural assumptions as by medical evidence. Despite a lack of evidence that underlying physical impairments have any relation at all to most cases of school failure,[15] in the United States the most common diagnoses given for children with reading difficulties are minimal brain dysfunction (MBD) or attention disorder. Both of these diagnoses are made by exclusion. A child who is having difficulty learning to read is subjected to physiological and psychological tests. If all these tests come back negative, the diagnosis is likely to be MBD. The reasoning is that if a child cannot read, there must be something organically or functionally wrong with his brain; otherwise, he would be able to read.

If it is assumed that children with learning disabilities are physically different from their normal peers, a sensible next step is to propose that they be separated from their peers and given special kinds of educational experiences. A realistic extension of this thinking is to assume that learning-disabled children are not the only ones who need special education. Would it not also be important to provide special programs designed to meet the needs of gifted children, children with emotional problems, hyperactive children, mildly retarded children, and children from many other categories?

The monetary cost of diagnosing children and providing special education programs is huge, and children placed in special education categories pay a high emotional cost in loss of motivation and estrangement from their peers. Although it may be true that being labeled learning disabled may cause a child to feel better about her poor performance in school, being told that she has a physical disorder may reduce her hope for improvement.

Special education has never been popular in Asia. Children

who would be in special education programs in the United States are routinely placed in mainstream Japanese and Chinese classrooms, and special classes or schools exist only for such demonstrably handicapped groups as blind, profoundly deaf, or severely retarded children. Why do Chinese and Japanese educators mainstream to this degree? Because they believe that the differences among children are not great enough to warrant the allocation of funds for special programs. High costs, both for the individual and for society, may result from expectations that are too low.

DEFINING THE PROBLEM

For the Asian cultures that we have studied, the goal of elementary school education is unambiguous: to teach children academic skills and knowledge—how to read, to write, to apply mathematics, to know something of history and government, and so on. Americans lack this clarity. Because of the belief that not every child is capable of mastering the academic curriculum, and because of a commitment to provide schooling for all children, Americans find it hard to decide what it is they expect from the nation's schools. One reason they are unwilling to define the goal of education narrowly as academic excellence is that they believe that only some children are capable of achieving it.

As an alternative, many Americans place a higher priority on life adjustment and the enhancement of self-esteem than on academic learning. They assume that positive self-esteem is a necessary precursor of competence. They forget that one of the most important sources of children's self-esteem is realizing that they have mastered a challenging task. What good is it for a third-grader—as was the case with the young daughter of one of our colleagues—to learn to copy the sentences, "I am Christy. I love and approve of myself," if she is incapable of writing her own sentences, of spelling, or of the other achievements of which third-graders are capable?

111

Tracking by ability, special education programs, and individualized instruction benefit some children, but they also produce the unintended consequence of depriving many children of opportunities to participate in normal classroom activities, thereby limiting their possibilities for learning. Our cross-cultural studies convince us that high average levels of achievement can be attained without the psychological and monetary costs of creating an educational system stratified on the basis of presumed ability.

Finally, the pervasive emphasis on innate ability lowers expectations about what can be accomplished through hard work. Whether children are considered to be bright or dull, the belief that ability is largely fixed leads parents and teachers to be reluctant to demand higher levels of performance from their children, and leads to a satisfaction with the status quo. Until Americans change their self-defeating beliefs about the limits that innate ability places on achievement, we have little hope for improving the quality of American education.

Chapter 6

Satisfactions and Expectations

The impetus for improvement lies in dissatisfaction with the way things are, and the current state of the educational system in the United States should give Americans plenty to be dissatisfied about. Yet our research indicates that dissatisfaction with American education may not be as widespread as the last decade's cries for reform might suggest. Social critics may be dissatisfied, but if educational reform is to succeed, dissatisfaction must extend to the American public, especially to the parents of children who attend the nation's schools. This apparently has not happened, and we must ask why.

Parents' satisfaction with their children's academic achievement and their children's schools depends only partially on the children's actual achievement. The same level of performance may leave some parents satisfied and others dissatisfied, depending on the standards and expectations they hold for their children. Standards and expectations, in turn, are strongly affected by cultural beliefs about the nature of human learning and potential. The belief that native ability limits academic achievement prevents many American parents from expecting excellence. If standards are too high, and more is expected of children than they are considered to be capable of, children's self-esteem could be damaged. To prevent this risk, Americans tend to adjust standards downward to a level considered to be appropriate for the child's level of ability.

Schools have used the self-esteem argument as one of the justifications for separating children into different tracks or ability groups. Standards guiding the expectations for children in the bottom tracks or groups are lowered, but we seldom see a corresponding increase in the demands made of children in the high tracks or groups. The curriculum as a whole is displaced downward in difficulty, so more children are regarded as doing quite well because standards are so low.

In this chapter we focus on parents' satisfactions with and expectations for their children and the education their children are receiving. The results add up to a very disturbing picture: highly satisfied American parents who apparently have little motivation for improving the quality of American education.

LEVELS OF SATISFACTION

We asked mothers in Minneapolis, Taipei, and Sendai whether they were *very satisfied, satisfied,* or *dissatisfied* with their children's performance in school. The percentage of mothers of first-graders who were "very satisfied" differed greatly among the three locations: 40 percent of American mothers but less than 5 percent of the Chinese and Japanese mothers said they were very satisfied. Four years later, when their children were in fifth grade, we interviewed the mothers again. The differences in their opinions were maintained: American mothers were more likely to be very satisfied with their children's schoolwork; Chinese and Japanese mothers were more likely to be dissatisfied (see Figure 6.1). A similar pattern appeared when we posed the same question to mothers in Chicago and Beijing: high satisfaction in Chicago and high dissatisfaction in Beijing.

FIGURE 6.1
Mothers' degree of satisfaction with their children's schoolwork when their children were in first and fifth grade.

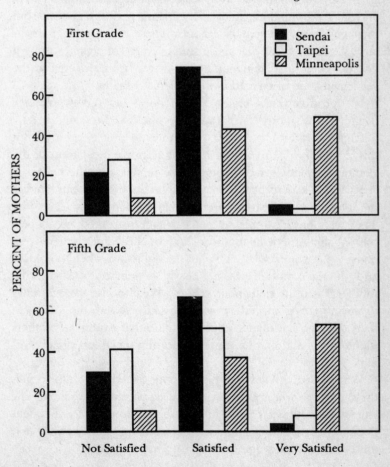

115

American parents' high level of satisfaction was not limited to their children's performance. They also expressed high satisfaction with how well the elementary schools were educating their children. Among Minneapolis mothers, 91 percent said their children's school was doing a good or excellent job; only around 40 percent of the Sendai and Taipei mothers rated their children's schools as favorably.

In all, we interviewed nearly three thousand mothers in five cities and our findings were consistent: American mothers were very satisfied with their children's academic performance and with their children's elementary schools. These findings are particularly startling, given that these studies were conducted during a decade when great national attention was being directed to the weakened state of education in the United States.

It is possible that Chinese and Japanese mothers simply give negative evaluations of whatever they are asked to rate, thereby making the ratings by American mothers seem very positive. But this is not likely. In contrast to their negative evaluation of the elementary schools, most Chinese and Japanese mothers (79 percent and 74 percent, respectively) in another of our studies thought the kindergartens were doing a good or excellent job. They were harder to please than the American mothers (95 percent of the American mothers thought the kindergartens were doing a good or excellent job), but the discrepancy between Asian and American mothers was not nearly so great as it was when the mothers rated the elementary schools. We interpret these findings to mean that Asian mothers were dissatisfied with the quality of their children's academic education, and that American mothers found their children's academic education much less disappointing.

Why are Americans so positive about the education their children get? We will argue that American parents, by holding low expectations for what their children can accomplish, form evaluations of their children's abilities and academic performance that are unrealistically high.

EVALUATIONS OF CHILDREN'S ABILITIES

J. Cannell, an educational researcher who studies national trends in achievement test scores,[1] reports that each of the fifty states describes its children, judged by test scores, to be above the national average. He termed this paradoxical finding the Lake Wobegon phenomenon, after the imaginary small town in Minnesota described by Garrison Keillor in his public radio program of the 1980s. Lake Wobegon is the idealization of the American hometown—"the little town that time forgot. Where all the women are strong, the men are good-looking, and all the children are above average." Keillor may have tapped something fundamental about the way Americans see themselves. Although half of all children must, by definition, be average or below, few Americans believe their own children fall into that category.

Intelligence and Personality

Most Americans perceive their children and themselves as being above average in many attributes—including intellectual abilities, favorable personality characteristics, and academic achievement. A few examples will illustrate our findings. We asked Taipei, Sendai, and Chicago mothers in one study to rate their children's intelligence, creativity, and memory on a five-point scale in which a rating of 3 was "average" and 5 was "much above average." Each mother was asked to compare her child with other children of the same age. Approximately 30 percent of the American mothers gave their children a 5—the highest rating on the scale—on all three attributes. Only about 10 percent of the Chinese and Japanese mothers gave their children ratings this high.

American parents also described their children's personality characteristics positively. Ratings of sociability, curiosity, creativity, persistence, and obedience were consistently higher for Ameri-

117

can than for Chinese and Japanese children. Conversely, American mothers did not describe their children as shy, anxious, or restless. Their impressions of themselves were also very positive, as reflected in high ratings of their own intelligence, memory, and learning abilities. American fathers were as likely as American mothers to be caught up in the Lake Wobegon effect. Their ratings of their children's intelligence, personality, and academic achievement were much more positive than the ratings made by Asian fathers.

Schoolwork

With great consistency, mothers in Chicago and Minneapolis thought their children were doing better in reading and mathematics than did their counterparts in Beijing, Sendai, and Taipei. They held positive views despite the fact that the national news media throughout the 1980s gave a great deal of attention to American children's academic deficiencies. If anything, the dire reports in the press may have heightened parents' tendency to hold a favorable view of their own children. *Other* children might be performing poorly and *other* schools might be failing, but these were not problems that most mothers discerned in their own situation.

American children shared their parents' optimism about how well they were doing in school. Chicago children gave themselves higher scores for achievement in reading and mathematics than did the Beijing children. When we asked Chicago first-graders how well they thought they would do in mathematics the following year, three fourths said they would be among the best students. Half or fewer of the Taipei and Sendai first-graders thought they would do so well. When we interviewed fifth-graders, we changed the question to ask how well they thought they would do in their high school mathematics courses. American students were very confident: 58 percent said they expected to be above average or among the best students. Little more than a quarter of the Chinese and Japanese fifth-graders gave themselves such high ratings.

Why Such High Ratings?

Do Americans really think very highly of themselves, or do they simply use the rating scales differently from Asians? Perhaps Americans just rate everyone high, not discriminating between high and low achievers. Or maybe ratings by American mothers appear high only because the ratings by Chinese and Japanese mothers are extremely low. Perhaps the Asian mothers are so modest and self-effacing that they hesitate to express the more positive opinions they actually hold. Such an interpretation is in line with Japanese and Chinese traditions of separating one's public position from one's private or "true" position. As a matter of politeness, a mother might deprecate her child's ability before others while at the same time truly believing that hers is an exceptional child.

We are able to test these possibilities by comparing the mothers' perceptions of their children's academic achievement with their children's actual test scores. If Americans are undiscriminating and Asians are excessively modest, there should be little relation between the way parents describe their children and the children's actual performance in any of the cultures. It turns out that mothers in Minneapolis, as well as those in Sendai and Taipei, had a reasonably accurate picture of where their children stood in relation to other children. Their ratings of their children's cognitive abilities paralleled the children's scores on a battery of ten cognitive tests, and their ratings of the children's reading and mathematics abilities followed roughly the same order as their children's scores on the achievement tests. Thus, mothers were able to evaluate their children's relative status among peers, and to do this effectively in all three cultures. What differed were the subjective labels mothers from the different societies placed on the scales. A level of performance described as "average" by Chinese and Japanese mothers was considered "above average" by American mothers.

We suggest, therefore, that the positive bias shown by Americans may represent a genuine tendency to overrate the actual level of performance, and that Asian mothers evaluate the level of their children's performance according to more stringent criteria. Alternatively, parents in America and Asia may know the truth about their children's performance, but the Americans hide their children's failures, while the Asians hide their children's successes.

SETTING STANDARDS

Does a positive bias imply that Americans are satisfied with low levels of performance? Does the more critical attitude of Chinese and Japanese parents result from more demanding standards? One way to answer these questions would be to look at the relation between children's achievement test scores and mothers' levels of satisfaction. If their standards are high, mothers should be pleased only by very high scores; they should be displeased by scores that show even modest signs of weakness. Mothers with lower standards should be satisfied more easily, and should be dissatisfied only when their children do quite badly.

We have the data to make these types of comparisons. We transformed each child's achievement score (combined scores on the reading and mathematics tests) into a percentile that indicated their level of performance relative to other children in their city. We then determined the average percentile of children whose mothers were dissatisfied, satisfied, or very satisfied with their children's level of achievement. These data appear in Figure 6.2.

The data are consistent with the argument that American mothers have lower standards than the Chinese and Japanese mothers. When the children were in first grade, there was little difference among the three cities in the percentiles associated with each level of maternal satisfaction. By the fifth grade, children of dissatisfied American mothers performed quite badly (below the 30th percentile), but children of dissatisfied Chinese and Japanese mothers were closer to the average in their achievement. Trends were just the opposite for the "very satisfied" mothers. Chinese

FIGURE 6.2
Children's academic achievement scores in first and fifth grade,
plotted according to their mothers' level of satisfaction.

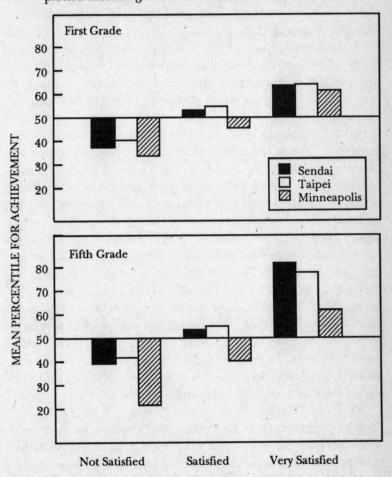

and Japanese children of these mothers were truly high achievers (above the 75th percentile); American children again were nearer the average. The children of "satisfied" American mothers were slightly below the average; those of Taipei and Sendai mothers were above average.

In short, American children could do worse relative to their peers before their mothers would be dissatisfied than Asian children could. Correspondingly, American mothers were satisfied or very satisfied with lower scores than were Chinese and Japanese mothers.

Perhaps even more surprising than the American mothers' low standards is the fact that their standards appeared to decline as their children proceeded from first to fifth grade. The basis for this conclusion can be seen by comparing the top and bottom panels of Figure 6.2. The average percentiles of the Chinese and Japanese children whose mothers reported being "very satisfied" were higher when the children were in fifth grade than when they were in first grade; those of the American children did not change over the four-year period. The converse is seen for the scores of children whose mothers were not satisfied. They declined in the case of the American children, but not for the Chinese and Japanese children. It seems, then, that during the course of elementary school Chinese and Japanese mothers required increasingly higher levels of achievement by their children in order to be very satisfied, but American mothers tolerated lower levels of achievement before they expressed dissatisfaction.

We assessed the standards held by parents in Beijing and Chicago by presenting them the hypothetical situation we described in Chapter 2: "Let's say your child took a math test for fifth-graders with 100 points. The average score was 70. What score do you think your child would get?" In estimating their children's grades, both Chinese and American mothers showed a positive bias: Mothers estimated that their children would receive an average score of 82 in Chicago and 85 in Beijing. After they had made their estimate, we asked them to tell us the least number of points with which they would be satisfied.

American mothers said they would be satisfied with scores that were *lower* than those they actually expected their children would receive. For Chinese mothers, the opposite occurred: They would be satisfied only if their children received *higher* grades than the ones they had predicted their children would make. American mothers of fifth-graders, for example, said they would be satisfied if their children made scores whose average was 76—six points lower than the average expected score. Chinese mothers would be satisfied only if their children made an average score of 94—nine points higher than the average they expected their children to make. The pattern was consistent for fathers as well as for mothers, and for estimates made for a reading test as well as for a math test.

These results are in line with a Chinese story that pokes fun at the high standards Chinese parents hold for their children. A Chinese mother is talking to her child: "What grade did you make on your reading test today in school? 93? If you had studied harder you would have been able to make 94." The child returns after the next week's test. "You made 94. You can do better than 94," suggests the mother. "Just spend a little more time at your studies." Finally, after weeks of study, the child proudly reports that her grade on this week's test was 100. "But will you be able to keep it up?" inquires the mother.

This story exaggerates the situation somewhat, but it is clear from our research that Chinese and Japanese parents do indeed hold high standards for their children's academic achievement, and that children accept these standards and work hard to meet them. American parents and children, by contrast, hold lower standards, and as a result, American children have less reason to study hard. Why should they spend a great deal of effort at their studies when just a little effort yields approval and praise? We should not be surprised that American children, satisfied with doing so little, fare poorly in their academic achievement compared to children from countries where standards are high and devotion to academic studies is strong.

WHY AMERICANS HAVE LOW STANDARDS

American parents face a number of serious impediments in judging the quality of their children's education. One of the strongest obstacles is the lack of clear external standards. American elementary schools generally do not provide grades; instead, they offer parents an evaluation of their children's progress made since the last report. Or the teacher may offer a broad classification such as *outstanding, satisfactory,* or *needs improvement.* Both types of report allow an optimistic evaluation of children's progress: Most children make some progress from term to term, and few are considered to be doing so badly that their parents need to be jarred by a "needs improvement" report.

The most specific information available to American parents comes from the results of state or national tests of educational progress. But these results, when made available at all, are often given in a form that is difficult to interpret. What does it mean, for example, when we read that a certain percentage of children within a school are passing at least three fourths of the items at the children's grade level? Does the score mean that the school is doing a good job or a poor job? If 60 percent of the students in Jackson School and 50 percent of the students in Lincoln School meet this criterion, should we be satisfied with the situation at either school?

American parents also find it difficult to know what they should expect from schools because we lack national performance goals that delineate what children are to learn in each grade. With no generally accepted guidelines, American parents cannot evaluate what is happening in their own children's schools. Adding to this difficulty is the American tendency to separate children into different classes or groups by presumed level of ability. It is impossible to know whether a child in the Bluebird reading group is really reading at an "average" level for first-graders—what is average

124

for the Bluebirds may be decidedly below average measured against the first-grade curriculum. The level is much more obvious when the whole class forms the basis for comparison. One of the most exasperating features of the separation of children into different levels within a grade is that the different textbooks they use often carry no information about the grade level for which the books are intended. Even if a parent looks over the child's textbook, he will not be able to judge the grade level for which it was written—unless he is a curriculum specialist.

Making informed judgments about schools is also made more difficult by the estrangement between parents and schools that has developed during the past several decades. There are many reasons for this estrangement, but the radical changes in elementary school curricula that began during the 1960s and that continue to be made are probably the greatest contributor. Many parents, faced with ever-changing approaches to math, science, and reading, are unfamiliar with what is being taught and rapidly come to perceive themselves as extraneous to the school-child relationship. At best, most parents participate in one or two conferences with the teacher and attend a few meetings of the parent-teacher association each year. Access to important sources of information about their children's education is thereby thwarted.

Chinese and Japanese parents get plenty of information about their children's education. There are daily homework assignments and frequent tests, and the parents know that homework and tests are based on textbooks reflecting the national curriculum. Communication between parents and teachers is also aided by the little notebooks the children carry home each day (described in Chapter 4) with notes from the teacher about homework or any problems that have arisen. As a consequence, Chinese and Japanese parents are better prepared to evaluate how the school and the child are faring at the tasks that have been prescribed for them.

The difficulty Americans have in adopting high standards is compounded by the fact that, in general, they do not place great emphasis on academic achievement. It is hard to maintain high standards about things that are not deemed to be of great importance. What may please the casual opera-goer may be scorned by the opera buff. Brazilians judge the quality of play in soccer by harsher standards than do Kansans. Education does not play as central a role in the American conception of the tasks and responsibilities of childhood as it does in Chinese and Japanese societies. According to most Asian parents, the major goal of childhood and adolescence is to obtain a good education, and as we have seen, families are dedicated to assisting their children in attaining this goal.

Being a good student is not foremost in the minds of most American children or their parents. Older American students often shy away from seeking distinction in their academic work because it isn't "cool," or because they fear they will be labeled nerds, grinds, or bookworms. Such attitudes make it easy for students who are "pretty good" at studies to be perceived, and to perceive themselves, as being good enough. If other aspects of life are more highly valued than doing well in school, it is unlikely that either parents or children will have a strong motivation to adopt high standards for academic achievement.

Nor are high standards likely to develop in an environment generally uncritical about issues concerning children. When we meet with our Japanese colleagues, the talk often turns to the problems in our respective school systems. As an example of the difference in scale of concern, in Japan, *ijime* (picking on and teasing another child) is regarded as a problem of national significance. Newspaper articles, special reports, and discussions at professional meetings deal with its prevalence and possible solutions. When we describe public school problems in the United States to our Asian colleagues, they are shocked. It is not uncommon in many large American cities for students to be physically attacked by other students, or for school authorities to take precautions to keep students from bringing knives and even guns to school. In Chicago, one reason given for the small number of recesses in some schools is that the neighborhoods are too dangerous for children to be out on the playground. There is no national outrage in the United States about these conditions. In fact, most citizens are unaware that they even exist. It takes a great deal of provocation for Americans to get worried about what is happening to their children. Americans would consider Japanese and Chinese parents to be worriers. Americans, on the other hand, have a strong tendency to understate their problems and to overstate their achievements.

These are all important reasons why Americans fail to impose higher standards on the accomplishments of the schools and their children, but there are other reasons as well. The past few decades have been difficult for many families in the United States. Large numbers of parents have so many problems of their own that they cannot be deeply concerned about academic excellence for their children. Demographic statistics about the family do not capture the extent to which their problems interfere with children's schoolwork. Regardless of whether a mother works, or whether a family is headed by one parent or two, raising children has become increasingly difficult for many families. Senator Jay Rockefeller, in his preface to the report of the National Commission on Children, summarizes the current status of American children and families in this way:

> America's enormous strengths and distressing weaknesses are nowhere more evident than in the lives of its children and families. Although many grow up healthy and happy in strong, stable families, far too many do not. They are children whose parents are too stressed and busy to provide caring attention and guidance. They are children who grow up without the material support and personal involvement of their mothers and fathers. They are children who enter school ill-prepared for the rigors of learning, who fail to develop the skills and attitudes needed to get good jobs and become responsible members of society.[2]

Many American parents also believe that this period is an especially difficult time for children in the United States and do

127

not wish to increase the pressure on their children by demanding high levels of performance in school. They often point to the presumed higher rates of suicide and emotional disturbance among Japanese adolescents as evidence for the validity of their worries. However, the belief that the pressures resulting from high standards have led to frequent suicide among Asian students is unfounded. In the 1950s, after World War II, the yearly rate of suicide by Japanese young people was above 30 per 100,000. Since that time the rate in Japan has dropped; currently, suicide by youths in both Japan and the United States occurs with a frequency of approximately 12 per 100,000.[3] There are no reliable statistics on emotional disturbance among children and adolescents by which the various societies can be compared, but we know of no evidence that Chinese or Japanese children are more prone to severe emotional disturbance than are American children.

DEFINING THE PROBLEM

One of the most sought-after goals in the world of marketing is a high degree of consumer satisfaction. But in the world of education, satisfaction by itself should not be the criterion for success. If both satisfaction and performance are high, we have cause for celebration. If satisfaction is high and performance is low, as is currently the case in the United States, we have cause for serious alarm.

The data that we have discussed pose an interesting problem. American parents, whose children generally score below Chinese and Japanese children on tests of academic achievement, gave the most positive evaluations when asked about their children's schools and how their children were performing. If the children were doing well, such high levels of satisfaction would be justified. But maintaining high levels of satisfaction with poor performance creates a huge obstacle to the improvement of education. Why should children study hard if their parents already express high levels of satisfaction? Why should schools pursue reform with enthusiasm and resolve when they already meet generally high levels of public approval? A high percentage of Americans are reluctant to examine the problems that we are sure to face in the coming decades if we continue to maintain the self-satisfied attitudes expressed by the parents and children we interviewed.

We Americans have historically had a high opinion of ourselves, with some justification. In only a few centuries we opened up a continent, established an effective political and economic system, and brought our nation unrivaled levels of prosperity. Americans have been thought of as courageous, industrious, and creative, an image we collectively have come to accept for ourselves. Nevertheless, a positive self-image is useful only to the extent that it is accurate. There is recent evidence that the basis for this positive image is eroding. To cling tenaciously to an unrealistically positive self-image breeds complacency, and even arrogance.[4]

The kinds of changes that are required in American education are unlikely to begin until optimistic approval is replaced by more appropriate levels of expectation. Americans want a good life for their children. They want their children to be happy and well adjusted. But to judge from our data, Americans as a society have not realized that access to the good life and happiness in the future will be blocked if we fail to prepare our children for the competition they will face in an ever more competitive world.

Chapter 7

The Organization
of Schooling

Imagine an elementary school with forty-five hundred students, like the largest one we visited in Taipei. Try to think of an educational system, like China's, that must serve more than 125 million elementary school children. Try to envision the changes that have taken place in Japan, where only 19 percent of the children attended junior high school in 1935, but nearly every child was enrolled in the mid-1980s. The numbers of students, the percentages attending school, and the sizes of the schools built to accommodate these enrollments are far beyond anything that we have experienced in the United States during the past half century.

Because of the large numbers of students and the surge in enrollment, elementary schools in Asia tend to be crowded, with many more children in a classroom than Americans would consider reasonable. Americans, who pay great attention to class size, would never believe that high levels of achievement are possible with classes of thirty-eight to fifty pupils, as was the case in the schools we visited. Large, academically successful classes are not the only surprise that awaits Westerners on their introduction to Chinese and Japanese schools. They are equally astonished by the schools' physical appearance and by the ways classes are organized and taught.

To understand children's academic achievement we must explore what happens at school more thoroughly than we have in earlier chapters. In this and the following two chapters, we describe the Chinese and Japanese schools, teachers, and teaching techniques and show how they shatter many American stereotypes about Asian education. By presenting a realistic picture of Asian schools, we gain a new perspective on American schools and on what may be required for them to be more effective.

PHYSICAL FACILITIES

One common American belief is that high levels of academic achievement are possible only in modern, well-equipped schools. This belief is rapidly destroyed when Americans look at the typical elementary school in China, or even in Taiwan and Japan. Asian governments invest more modestly in buildings and equipment than does the United States. School buildings are austere, built to be functional rather than comfortable. Their dullness is relieved mainly by the children's bright faces and colorful displays of their artwork. Furnishings are sparse, and space, which is at a premium throughout Asia, is used with maximum efficiency.

Schools in China are the most spartan. The majority have been hastily constructed and minimally equipped, and they are poorly maintained. There is little heating in most schools, and classroom windows often remain open even in the middle of winter. Children and teachers combat the cold by wearing multiple layers of clothing. The crowded classrooms contain little more than a small desk at the front of the room for the teacher and rows of desks for

131

the children. A blackboard, a battered public-address speaker, and a small shelf of well-used books typically complete the furnishings.

In Taipei, schools must accommodate a population that has outgrown the available physical facilities. Many schools are located in busy sections of the city where heavy traffic produces a high noise level outside the classrooms. Equipment has improved during the past few years as the economy has developed, but a high-tech classroom is hard to find. Teaching materials are usually constructed by the teachers, and their most advanced equipment is usually an overhead projector.

The situation is somewhat different in Japan, where the financial boom of the past three decades has increased the availability of funds for education. Schools are well maintained; many classrooms have television sets, and teachers have ready access to excellent teaching materials. Even so, we have yet to encounter an elementary school in Japan with the amenities that many school administrators in the United States consider to be necessities, such as central heating, spacious classrooms, a school library, comfortable cafeterias, well-equipped gymnasiums, and computer rooms. Although such schools may exist in Japan, school administrators seldom aspire to these luxuries. The library corners, displays of plants and animals, and work areas common to classrooms in American elementary schools are seldom included in plans for Japanese classrooms.

When older American adults visit Asian schools, they often remark that the schools remind them of the ones they attended when they were children. Asian schools do resemble those built in the United States forty or fifty years ago, when in order to meet the expanding demand for public education, construction was dictated by service rather than comfort. Like many of today's schools in Asia, older American schools consisted of little more than classrooms, each arranged in a standard pattern: rows of desks for the children facing the teacher's desk at the front.

SUPPORT FOR EDUCATION

Educators all over the world decry the inadequacy of the financial support for elementary and secondary schools. Complaints are heard in China as frequently as in the United States. In 1988, for example, the Chinese vice minister of the state education commission lamented the "insufficient funds, poor school conditions, [and] low pay for teachers" in China. China devotes 3.7 percent of its gross national product to education—a modest amount compared to the 6.8 percent of the much larger GNP in the United States.[1]

The money available for education is allocated differently in Asia and in the United States. Besides the lower expenditures for buildings and furnishings, Asian ministries of education allocate little money to nonteaching positions. Administrative staffs of even the largest Asian schools are small; there are few janitors and service personnel; one rarely encounters special education teachers; there are no assistant teachers, school psychologists, counselors, or social workers. Our Asian colleagues are perplexed about why we spend so much money on janitors, for example, when children can help keep the school clean and the money could be better used for activities that support the primary purpose of education—classroom learning. Is not the family, the Asian parent asks, responsible for handling children's emotional problems, rather than the school? Should not the parents, rather than special teachers, assist slow learners? Funds not spent on physical facilities and nonteaching personnel can be devoted to teachers' salaries. This may be part of the reason why teaching in elementary schools is a more attractive occupation in Asia than in the United States. In Japan, for example, a prospective teacher is not lured away by Mitsubishi or Toyota because of the promise of a higher salary. Elementary school teachers and corporation employees with comparable degrees of education receive equivalent salaries.

133

GOALS OF EDUCATION

Decisions about a nation's schools appear to be determined by commonly held assumptions about the goals of education rather than by the nation's political philosophy. Educators in Communist China and in capitalist Japan and Taiwan agree that regardless of an individual child's proclivities or interests, all children need to acquire certain basic information and fundamental skills. They believe that all children can benefit from a common educational experience, and that to provide different experiences to different children could lead to inequities that would later make it difficult for some children to compete for jobs. The goal of education, we were told by a Japanese education official, "is the reduction of individual differences among children." Most Asian educators share this view; most Americans reject it.

American educators emphasize the importance of individual differences, an emphasis deeply rooted in American culture, and their commonly held goal for education is to maximize each child's potential. American philosophers of education, adhering to a more nativist philosophy than their Chinese and Japanese counterparts, emphasize discovering the characteristics and needs of each child and then constructing educational experiences that respond to these individual needs. Howard Gardner, a representative of this position, summarizes it: "A most important event in a child's education is the discovery of a domain of strength and interest. Once this area has been found, the student can be expected to thrive; and if it has not been found the student may well never appreciate the excitement of learning."[2]

Chinese and Japanese believe that it is unnecessary to consider individual differences in setting curricular goals and in devising educational programs. They argue that members of their ministries of education have a good understanding of what children need to know in order to adapt successfully to society and of how to organize experiences that will promote learning. Moreover, they point out that only through a central ministry of education is it possible to ensure that regardless of the schools they attend, all children will be exposed to the same curriculum, will be taught by teachers following very similar approaches to teaching, and will be expected to meet the same general criteria of performance.

The occupation of Japan after World War II illustrates the vast differences in the American and Japanese attitudes toward central control of education. The American occupation forces called in a group of American experts to help them reform Japanese schools. The American consultants voiced strong support for a system of local control, contending that children's potential is more likely to be maximized when the schools are run by persons familiar with the characteristics and needs of the local population. They recommended that the Japanese abandon centralized control and distribute authority, American style, to local school boards. Thousands of school boards were created, and they attempted to function for several years. Nevertheless, as soon as the American occupation ended, the Japanese quickly reverted to their former pattern of central control through the Ministry of Education, Science, and Culture (Monbusho). The prior dispersion of control was criticized as leading to inequities. Without central control, Japanese educators argued, there was no way to guarantee that teachers would be aware of what the children had been taught in earlier grades, that all children would share a common fund of knowledge and skills, and that children would not be penalized when their parents moved from one school district to another.

Americans also began to be aware of some of the negative outcomes of decentralization. The strong emphasis on local control of schools had produced great inequalities in children's opportunities for a decent education. Some children, because of their race or their socioeconomic status, were forced to attend segregated schools or schools that could not pay an adequate staff. The federal government, reacting to these inequities, attempted to promote greater equality of opportunity through federal supervision of policies concerning segregation, special education, and employment. Schools now face the threat of withdrawal of federal funds if they do not comply with the policies. When it comes to ensuring equity among their children through central control of the curriculum, however, Americans have been reluctant to allow the federal government to assume this power.

CONTROL OF THE CURRICULUM

Visiting a number of classrooms at the same grade level and at the same time of year in a city like Taipei gives one an intense feeling of déjà vu. All fifth-graders within the school, within different schools in the city, even within all of Taiwan, are studying the same lesson. Whether it is reading about Iceland, learning new Chinese characters, or finding out how to calculate the volume of a cube, the same material will be covered more or less on the same day of the school year. This uniformity is a result of the central control of the curriculum by the Ministry of Education, which specifies in great detail the order and content of what shall be taught.

The ministries of education in both Taiwan and Japan publish volumes describing the course of study in elementary schools. The general objectives of instruction for each subject at each grade are described in three or four paragraphs, followed by detailed descriptions of the content of the curriculum. In Japan's curriculum for fourth-grade mathematics, for example, seventeen sections describe what is to be accomplished in five main content areas: numbers and calculation, quantities and measurement, geometric figures, quantitative relations, and terms and symbols.

Specification of the curriculum does not stop at the description of the content, but extends to a detailed schedule of how many hours are to be devoted to each subject throughout elementary school. In China, for example, children attend classes thirty-four hours a week in grades one through six. During this time, reading is to occupy a minimum of ten hours; mathematics, six; natural science, from two to three; arts and music, two each; physical education from two to three; and moral education, one. Slight variations, depending on the grade, exist in the subjects that are included and in the amount of time spent on each.

The United States does not have a national curriculum. Every state, and at times every school district within a state, is responsible for devising its own curriculum. Some argue that this is the only way to meet the needs of children residing in different parts of the country. This may be true, but the lack of a national curriculum has negative consequences. Enormous diversity in what is taught in the nation's schools and the fact that not all children have access to a basic core of knowledge and skills means that large numbers of young Americans cannot compete for future employment or participate fully as citizens.

Although there has been strong resistance in the United States to having a standard national curriculum, the potential contribution of national curricular guidelines is beginning to be discussed as the need for educational reform has become apparent. Federal guidelines concerning the integration of schools and the distribution of funds have not been sufficient to guarantee equal educational opportunity, and it is being suggested that federal intervention will be necessary to remedy this situation. Proponents of national guidelines point out that a national consensus about the goals for some subjects, such as mathematics and physical sciences, is readily attainable. After all, everyone agrees that children need to learn how to add and multiply, to understand gravity and chemical reactions. But there are other subjects, such as social studies, civics, and biology, for which the goals provoke angry debate. Even language arts has been a controversial subject, for opinions vary widely about what should be read, written, or discussed in these classes.

In defining the national goals for education, President Bush and the state governors recently urged the National Assessment Governing Board "to begin work to set national performance goals."[3]

Although they were quick to disavow that establishing such goals would result in increasing federal control over the curriculum, it nevertheless seems likely that in pursuing this charge some type of national guidelines is likely to emerge. This move toward a national curriculum will probably be welcomed by many people: In 1989, a surprising 69 percent of adults contacted in the twenty-first annual Gallup Poll favored requiring public schools to use a standardized national curriculum. Only 21 percent were opposed.[4]

TEXTBOOKS

In order to implement national guidelines, the national government must inevitably have some influence on the content of children's textbooks. This influence has taken different forms in Asia. In Taiwan, every textbook is written under the direct supervision of the Ministry of Education. Complete uniformity in all schools is accomplished by providing a single textbook series for each subject. In Taiwan, and also in China, the governments themselves publish all the textbooks used in the schools, thereby guaranteeing that their content adheres to the standard curriculum. In China, with its huge population, regional governments may produce different textbook series, so the textbooks used in Shanghai or Guangzhou are not necessarily the same as those used in Beijing. Nevertheless, the content of all textbooks is the responsibility of the government, and textbooks throughout China must cover essentially the same material.

In Japan, textbooks are produced by private publishing companies, but they must meet the guidelines defined by the Monbusho. The choice of textbooks, typically made by educational administrators in the prefecture, is not especially difficult. A relatively small number of companies dominate the textbook market, and the various textbook series differ primarily in their superficial features, such as how problems are presented and the order in which concepts are developed.

The open market in the United States has resulted in a profusion of textbooks for every subject taught in school. The market is enormous, and both large and small publishing houses compete fiercely to get their textbooks adopted. There is no consistent system throughout the country for adopting textbooks. Some state governments exert control, but in other states the choice is left to local school districts, to individual schools, or even to the individual teacher. Because the content of the textbooks sometimes differs widely, the adoption of a new series is often a source of much controversy and wrangling by teachers, school boards, and state governments.

General Features of Textbooks

Textbooks published in Japan, Taiwan, and China bear little physical resemblance to the typical American elementary school textbooks. Asian textbooks are slim, inexpensively produced paperbacks. Separate volumes, seldom containing more than one hundred pages, cover each semester's work in each subject. The covers are attractive, but the inside pages have few illustrations and are devoted primarily to text. Illustrations tend to depict only the central point of the lesson, and there is very little information that is not necessary for the development of the concepts under consideration. They present the essence of the lesson, with the expectation that the teacher will elaborate and supplement the information with other materials.

American textbooks, in contrast, are thick, hard-cover volumes covering a whole year's work. There are colorful illustrations, photographs, drawings, or figures on nearly every page. This artwork, along with digressions into historical and biographical material, is introduced to engage children's interest, but may instead distract attention from the central purpose of the lesson.

Another distinguishing feature of American textbooks is the importance the writers place on repetition and review, features that they know adoption committees will require. The textbooks follow what is often described as a spiral curriculum. At each grade level they present materials related to many different topics, and they repeat the discussion with some elaboration at later grades. Daunted by the length of most textbooks and knowing that the children's future teachers will be likely to return to the material, American teachers often omit some topics. Different topics are omitted by different teachers, thereby making it impossible for the children's later teachers to know what has been covered at earlier grades—they cannot be sure what their students know and what they do not. Asian textbooks, by contrast, are developed on the assumption that knowledge should be cumulative from semester to semester; if the concept or skill is taught well the first time, it is unnecessary at a later grade to repeat the discussion.

Content of Textbooks

We found little indication in our detailed analyses of Asian and American textbooks that one set of textbooks was more difficult than the other, despite their differences in general appearance and in their approach to the material in the elementary school curriculum. Textbooks in reading introduce about the same number of different words by the end of elementary school—roughly seven thousand in the series used in Taiwan, Japan, and the United States. Mathematics textbooks included about the same number of concepts and skills—for example, of the 497 concepts and skills that appeared in the Japanese and American textbooks combined, 83 percent were introduced in the Japanese textbooks and 82 percent in the American textbooks.

Nevertheless, there is a substantial difference between Japanese and American textbooks in the explicitness with which the concepts are discussed. Japanese textbooks often are less explicit, especially in mathematics. For example, addition of two three-digit numbers involving carrying never appears in Japanese textbooks, although later problems clearly assume children have learned how to add them. Japanese textbook writers depend on the teacher to assist children with discussion and elaboration of the content of the lesson more than American authors do.

It is also apparent that Japanese textbook writers seek to engage children's active participation to a greater degree than American writers believe is necessary or possible. If all the steps in the application of a concept or skill are presented, as in American textbooks, children must simply follow the argument, without encountering gaps that they must figure out for themselves. Since one goal of Asian teachers is to have children learn that there are many different methods for solving problems, presenting a single method in such full detail would limit the likelihood that children would come up with alternative solutions. A common technique used by Asian teachers in mathematics classes is to have children present as many different solutions to a problem as possible, and then to have the class discuss which methods are most efficient, and why.

The influence of textbooks on educational practices depends on how exhaustively their content is used by teachers. One gets the impression that few American teachers expect to cover all aspects of every chapter in the textbook. Not only are large sections within chapters skipped, but the teacher may omit whole chapters. This is not the case in Chinese and Japanese classrooms. Textbooks that contain short lessons, a limited number of practice problems, and practically no ancillary material make it possible for the class to cover every detail contained in every textbook. Through notes taken in class, class exercises, and homework, every child will have had to attend to every word, every problem, and every exercise included in every textbook used during elementary school.

TIME AT SCHOOL

Much has been made of the longer school day and the longer school year in Asian schools. "American students are falling behind their peers abroad—maybe because they get less schooling," proclaimed the cover of the November 1990 issue of *The Atlantic Monthly* magazine. It is true that Chinese and Japanese children finish the sixth grade having spent the equivalent of one to two years longer at school than American children. The Asian school day is longer, and there are more days in each school year. These are impressive statistics, but their implications are not as simple as they first appear.

Schools in Taiwan and China follow a yearly schedule similar to that of the United States, except that they remain in session longer in the summer. School begins in early September and ends in July. There is a break in December and a later one at the time of the Chinese New Year. In Japan, the school year is divided into three terms: April through July, September through December, and January through March. All Chinese and Japanese schools are in session every day but Sunday during these periods. These schedules result in 240 days of school per year in Chinese and Japanese elementary schools. American schools are in session only 180 days a year.

Most Asian schools follow very similar daily schedules. Beijing can serve as an example. Children arrive at school between eight and eight-thirty in the morning, and depart for home around four in the afternoon, except on Saturdays, when they leave school at noon. The day is divided into four forty-five or fifty-minute classes in the morning and two in the afternoon. After formal classes are over, children spend an hour or more at school in extracurricular activities. We estimate that second- through sixth-graders in Chinese classrooms spend between 1400 and 1700 hours a year in school. First-graders typically have a shorter daily schedule, which reduces the hours to approximately 1100.

The daily schedule is much different for American children, who typically arrive at school around nine and leave before three. They spend approximately 1100 hours a year at school. It would appear, therefore, that Chinese children spend something between 1500 and 3000 more hours at elementary school—the equivalent of one to two years of school life—than the American children. (These estimates come from subtracting the 1100 hours of the American second- through sixth-graders from the corresponding 1400 to 1700 hours of the Chinese children, and multiplying by five years.)

Statistics such as these have convinced many Americans that extending the length of the school day and of the school year is a necessary first step in the improvement of American education. When we look more closely at the statistics, however, the argument for more time in school is weakened. It is often forgotten that the estimate of 240 days includes Saturdays, when Asian children are in school only a half day. This reduces the number of days in the Asian school year by the equivalent of twenty days.

A further correction must be made for the amount of time at school spent in recess, lunch, and after-school extracurricular activities, as contrasted with academic classes. The schedules in Beijing and Chicago are typical. We estimate that Beijing children spend an average of fifty minutes a day in recesses, versus ten minutes provided by the Chicago schools. As much as an hour and a half is devoted to lunch in Beijing—more than three times what is allowed in most American schools. After-school activities, which normally take place outside school in the United States, keep most Beijing children occupied at school for an hour or two a day after their regular classes are over. So although Asian children spend more time at school than American children, the difference in the amount of academic instruction is not so profound as the more general statistics imply.

Perhaps more important than the total amount of time spent in school is the way in which this time is distributed throughout the year. In contrast to the two-day weekends and long summer vacations that provide discontinuities in the American school year, time flows more or less continuously in Chinese and Japanese schools. School vacations in Asia are shorter and spaced more evenly throughout the year. Learning is an unceasing process, maintained by the momentum developed during regular classes.

Adding to this momentum are the opportunities Asian children have during vacations for practice and review. Asian schools are not "open" during vacation periods. But this does not mean that they cease to function. Except for their own brief vacations, Chinese and Japanese teachers are at school throughout the year.

Children, too, are seldom away from their neighborhoods, for families in Asia rarely take vacation trips together. Throughout vacation periods, clubs and activity groups continue to meet, children may continue to receive homework assignments from their teachers, and new academic projects are begun. In these ways Asian students do have a longer "school" year, but much of the additional time is not spent in the regular classroom.

CLASSROOM ORGANIZATION

Our information about how classrooms function comes from several large observational studies that we have conducted over the past decade. In one study our observers were in classrooms for a total of more than four thousand hours—more than a thousand class periods in twenty first- and twenty fifth-grade classrooms in each of three cities (Minneapolis, Sendai, and Taipei). Observers coded the presence or absence of predetermined categories of behavior throughout each class period. From this enormous amount of data we are able to describe classroom activities in the three cultures with high precision. The following examples rely on observations made in mathematics classes, although the findings were very similar for the other academic classes we visited.

Elementary school classrooms are typically organized in one of three ways: The whole class is working as a unit; the class is divided into a number of small groups; or children are working individually. In our observations we noted when the child was receiving instruction or assistance from the teacher and when the child was working on his own. He was considered to be receiving instruction whenever the teacher was the leader of the activity, whether it involved the whole class, a small group, or only the individual child.

Looking at the classroom in this manner led us to one of our most striking findings: Although the number of children in Asian classes was much greater than the number in American classes, Asian students received more instruction from their teachers than did American students. In Taiwan, the teacher was the leader of the child's activity 90 percent of the time, as opposed to 74 percent in Japan, and only 46 percent of the time in the United States. No one was leading instruction 9 percent of the time in Taiwan, 26 percent in Japan, and an astonishing 51 percent of the time in the United States (see Figure 7.1). Even American first-graders actually spent more time on their own than they did participating in an activity led by the teacher.

FIGURE 7.1
Percentage of time the child's activity was led by
the teacher and by no one.

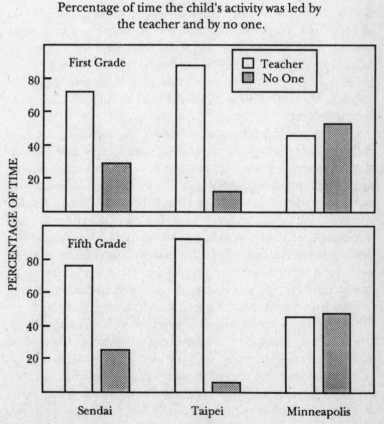

One of the reasons American children received less instruction is that American teachers spent 13 percent of their time in the mathematics classes not working with any students, something that happened only 6 percent of the time in Japan and 9 percent in Taiwan. (As we will see later, American teachers have to steal class time to attend to the multitude of chores involving preparation, assessment, and administration because so little nonteaching time is available for them during the day.)

A much more critical factor in the erosion of instruction was the amount of time American teachers were involved with individuals or small groups. American children spent 10 percent of their time in small groups and 47 percent of their time working individually. Much of the 87 percent of the time American teachers were working with their students was spent with these individual students or small groups, rather than with the class as a whole. When teachers provide individual instruction, they must leave the rest of the class unattended, so instructional time for all remaining children is reduced.

Children can learn without a teacher. Nevertheless, it seems likely that they could profit from having their teacher as the leader of their activities more than half the time they are in the classroom. One might argue that skill in subjects such as reading is highly dependent on practice and that children benefit from reading by themselves or in small groups. It is more difficult to defend this argument for subjects such as mathematics and science, where children may need more direct instruction before they can profit from studying by themselves. It is the incredibly large amounts of time that American children are left unassisted and the effect that unattended time has on the lesson that is the problem.

Since Asian students spend so much of their time in whole-group work, we need to say a word about that format. Whole-class instruction in the United States has gotten a somewhat bad reputation. It has become associated with too much teacher talk and too many passive, tuned-out students. But as we will see in more detail as we continue our description of Asian classrooms, whole-class instruction in Japanese and Chinese classrooms is a very lively, engaging enterprise. Asian teachers do not spend large amounts of time lecturing. They present interesting problems; they pose provocative questions; they probe and guide. The students work hard, generating multiple approaches to a solution, explaining the rationale behind their methods, and making good use of wrong answers.

Dividing Time

We planned our observations so that they would occur only during academic classes, and not during recess, gym, assemblies, or lunch. Being in an academic class is not necessarily equivalent, however, to being involved in an academic activity. Time may be lost in many ways: The lesson may begin late or stop early, the teacher may be called out of the room, or the children may be in transition from one academic activity to another.

American children spent the least amount of time actually engaged in academic activities in academic classes: 70 percent of the time in first grade, followed by a decline to 65 percent in fifth grade. These data contrast sharply with those obtained for the Asian children. The corresponding data for the Chinese and Japanese children actually rose between first and fifth grades. The percentage increased for the Chinese children from an already high 85 percent to an even higher 92 percent, and for the Japanese children, from 79 percent to 87 percent. If much of the time in academic classes taught in American elementary schools is essentially wasted, would it not be sensible to institute procedures for making these classes more efficient before we consider lengthening the amount of time children spend in school?

Some procedures could be changed with little expense. For example, American children do not know how to move efficiently from one activity to another: finding their textbooks and then locating the page the class is to read, or trying to find a sharpened pencil or a clean sheet of paper. Minneapolis children in both first and fifth grades spent much more time in such transitions than did Sendai and Taipei children. Minneapolis fifth-graders, for example, spent roughly 10 percent of the time they were in academic classes in transition; Sendai and Taipei children, about 5 percent and 6 percent respectively. So American children wasted about 5 percent of the time they were in school waiting for other children.

Additional time was lost in the American classrooms in irrelevant activities that could be minimized if children were taught to use their time constructively. American children spent more time out of their seats, talked more to their peers at inappropriate times, and engaged in other inappropriate activities to a greater degree than did the Chinese and Japanese children. For example, American fifth-graders were out of their seats nearly 20 percent of the time; Chinese and Japanese fifth-graders, less than 5 percent. Activities in which children are "off-task" are a source of frustration and tension in American classrooms. Greater time off-task, together with inefficient transitions, make American classrooms appear disorganized.

Data such as these led one of our Japanese colleagues to praise American children's academic achievement. Don't American children do remarkably well, he proposed, when one considers how little of their time they spend in academic activities, how little instruction they receive from their teachers, and how few opportunities they have for out-of-classroom practice?

Curriculum. All the schools teach language arts (reading, writing, and spelling), mathematics, social science, music, and art. Taipei and Sendai schools also have classes in moral education, which attempt to inculcate values and practices that demonstrate respect, fairness, rationality, and other attributes of a good citizen and family member. Physical and biological sciences are seldom taught in the elementary schools of any of the cities we visited.

Deciding which subject is being taught in a class would seem to be easy, but it was not always a simple task in the loosely organized American classrooms. Our observers sometimes found it impossible to decide and had to solicit the opinion of the teacher. The schedule was much more easily discerned in Chinese and Japanese classrooms. Each class period is designed for the presentation of a lesson, which in every case is a lesson in a particular subject.

First-grade teachers in all three cultures made reading their primary focus of attention, reflecting the widespread recognition that children who are unable to read can benefit little from other areas of elementary school education. At first grade, as is evident in Figure 7.2, mathematics received the most attention in Sendai and the least in Minneapolis. In fifth-grade classrooms, language arts continued to dominate class time in Minneapolis, but not in Sendai or Taipei, where approximately equal amounts of time were spent on reading and mathematics.

FIGURE 7.2
How classroom time is spent on various subjects.

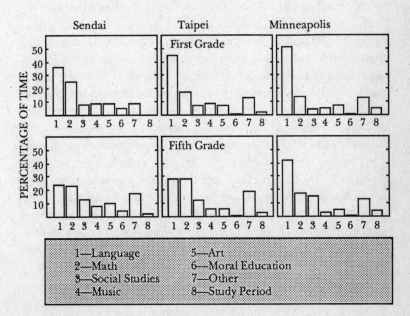

When the percentages of time spent in reading and mathematics were plotted separately by individual classroom, we found much greater variability among the Minneapolis classrooms than among those in Taipei or Sendai. Some Minneapolis teachers spent as much as 40 percent of their time teaching mathematics; several others never taught mathematics in the twenty randomly chosen hours when our observers visited each classroom. Variability among classrooms was low in Sendai and Taipei, undoubtedly because the national curriculum clearly specified how much time should be spent in teaching each subject.

The difference in the ways Asian and American teachers divide their instructional time between reading and mathematics surely has many causes, but an important one is that American teachers like to teach reading; Asian teachers like to teach mathematics. When we asked teachers in Beijing, nearly all of whom were women, the subject they most liked to teach, 62 percent said mathematics, 29 percent said language arts. The reverse was found in Chicago: 33 percent mentioned mathematics and 47 percent mentioned language arts. There is more to the story than preference, however. Americans simply emphasize reading more than mathematics. Despite the large amount of time already spent in reading instruction, more than 40 percent of the suggestions made by Minneapolis mothers who wanted an increased emphasis on academic subjects said they thought that the subject should be reading. Fewer than 20 percent mentioned mathematics.

These data lead to the obvious conclusion that American children do less well in mathematics than do Chinese and Japanese children partly because they spend less time studying mathematics. Although time itself cannot completely explain their poor performance, the small amount of class time and the time wasted in transitions and irrelevant behavior must be important factors. Conversely, American children may fare better in reading, relatively speaking, because they spend more time on this subject.

TRACKING

An Asian family enrolling a child in elementary school has no choice of school. School assignment is determined by the neighborhood in which the family resides. Nor has the parent any choice in the child's assignment to a teacher. All assignments are random. Other than seeking to have an equal number of boys and girls in each classroom, no constraints are placed on who goes into what class. Parents can always choose to enroll the child in a private school, of course, but the procedure for assigning children to classes in private schools is the same as in public schools.

Tracking does not exist in Asian elementary schools. Children are never separated into different classrooms according to their presumed levels of intellectual ability.[5] The egalitarian philosophy carries over to organization within the classroom. Children are not separated into reading groups according to their ability; there is no division of the class into groups differentiated by the rate at which they proceed through their mathematics books. No children leave the classroom for special classes, such as those designed for children diagnosed as having learning disabilities.

Schools in the United States are organized to meet what are perceived to be the individual needs of each child. Within classrooms, it is assumed that individual differences among children are so great that it is necessary to divide the classroom into separate groups, each proceeding through the curriculum at a different rate. Children who have been diagnosed as having intellectual, emotional, or educational disabilities are assigned to special programs or attend special classes part of every day.

From the time American parents first encounter the school system, they are confronted with the fact that not all children are considered to be equally capable of benefitting from participation in regular classroom activities. Beginning when they bring their five-year-olds to kindergarten roundup, as the registration for kindergarten is termed in many parts of the country, parents are faced with the question of what type of class would best serve their children. During the roundup, hearing and vision are tested to see if the children have any physical handicaps that should be taken into account. There is also a brief psychological screening. The goal of the screening tests is to ascertain whether a child is intellectually and socially ready for school.

For many years the American emphasis on meeting children's needs by assigning them to different educational tracks from the time they enter elementary school was accepted as educationally and psychologically sound. More recently it has come under criticism. Critics charge that tracking creates a categorization of students that is usually unnecessary and sometimes unhealthy. The excessively large percentage of minority children assigned to special education classes, the denial of access to the regular curriculum for children assigned to certain categories, and the stigma that children feel in being separated from their peers have been cited as reasons to change the way schools and classrooms are currently organized.

DEFINING THE PROBLEM

Educators in the United States, reflecting the values of American society, seek to meet the special needs of every child. Asians make few concessions to individual differences among children, but devote their energies to raising the general level of achievement. Americans respond to individual differences by assigning slow or fast learners to special classes or by grouping children within classrooms according to their presumed learning ability. Only in the most extreme cases are Asian children segregated from their peers.

Each approach has its strengths and weaknesses. Critics point out that the child who learns slowly is at a serious disadvantage in a system where every student is expected to master each day's lessons. Even Asian teachers acknowledge that some children get further and further behind their classmates the longer they remain in school. Children who have special skills or abilities are held back when there is no provision for studying any but prescribed textbooks or for solving problems more complex than those appearing in the standard curriculum. From the American perspective these are serious problems. Asians may acknowledge that such problems exist, but prefer educational practices that benefit the greatest number of students. They point to the high average performance level of their children as an index of the effectiveness of this strategy.

The enormous emphasis in American schools on individual differences has also produced many problems. The creation of classes for children with special needs and the strong desire to have small numbers of children in all classrooms impose an enormous drain on resources available for education. American schools, as they are currently funded, may be unable to meet all the needs of all children, and it seems unlikely that many of the functions with which they have been charged during the past several decades can be maintained without further deterioration of our educational system. Attempts to help children with special problems not only strain available financial resources but also pose costs for the children themselves. We identify children as needing special help in their early days of schooling, segregate them into special classrooms or special groups, and label them as reading disabled, emotionally impaired, or hyperactive. But we have not yet devised humane ways of helping these children handle their difficulties without forcing them to bear the stigma of being labeled as impaired, disabled, or deviant early in their lives.

A serious impediment to achieving equal opportunities for all children is the great variation in the content of the curriculum followed in different American classrooms. Teachers are allowed to emphasize or de-emphasize subjects, depending upon their own interests and what is demanded by parents. In mathematics, for example, teachers confess a lack of interest in the subject, parents de-emphasize its importance, and the time different teachers devote to mathematics varies widely. Large discrepancies in what children have studied may lead to severe problems when children transfer to a new school or when they are called upon to use skills that they have not been taught by a previous teacher.

The uneven quality of the books and materials available to American students poses a closely related problem. Compared to textbooks used in Asia, American textbooks are often overwhelming in size, distracting in format, and redundant from year to year. Workbooks repeat, rather than enhance, what the children have already covered, and few children have access to hands-on materials that could help them to translate abstract concepts into concrete everyday experiences.

There are also problems with the way educational funds are allocated in the United States. It is clear that American schools allocate too much of their current resources to administration, nonteaching personnel, and physical facilities. In addition, universities and colleges, which serve only a portion of the population, receive a high proportion of all educational funds. This pattern of expenditure has resulted in a system of higher education that is equal to or superior to that of any other country in the world, but it may also have contributed to weakening elementary and secondary education.

It is not the case, however, that a reallocation of funds from colleges and universities to primary and secondary schools would make the nation more competitive. A decrease in the capacity of universities to generate scientific advances may jeopardize our status as an economic power in an era when technological advances are necessary for competition and survival. Transfer of funds from colleges and universities to elementary and secondary schools would surely lead to such a decrease. On the other hand, universities would function more effectively and the work force of the country would be strengthened if students acquired greater competence in language arts, mathematics, and science during their elementary and secondary education.

Finally, American schools operate inefficiently. Schools suffer from frequent disarray, disorganization, and unproductive use of time. How can this fail to be the case as long as teachers are given little free time for preparation, for working with individual students, and for all the managerial tasks that have become their responsibility?

Chapter 8

The Profession of Teaching

Just as parents play a central role in fostering children's learning and development at home, teachers are critical in determining the shape of children's lives at school. It is natural, then, that in our quest to understand children's academic performance we turn our attention to teachers: who they are, how they are trained, and how their jobs are organized.

Elementary school teachers in the societies we have studied have much in common. Except for Sendai, where nearly half the teachers were men, most were women, and most had been at their jobs for a long time (an average of sixteen to twenty years). Despite the problems that are known to plague their profession, American as well as Chinese and Japanese teachers reported that they would choose teaching as a career again if they had it to do over. Why did they choose to become teachers in the first place? The number one reason given in all three cultures was the desire to work with children. Salary, prestige, working conditions, time off in the summer—all were judged to be less important. The teachers simply liked teaching children.

Enjoyment of teaching young children is important, but being a successful teacher requires more than that. When we compare the ways that teachers are trained and the nature of the teaching profession in American and Asian societies, it quickly becomes clear that despite being faced with an incredibly arduous and demanding task, American teachers are inadequately trained. Furthermore, they often lack the support and cooperation of parents and society, the social status and financial compensation commensurate with the importance of their job, and, perhaps above all, opportunities for personal development.

BECOMING A TEACHER

Americans often act as if good teachers are born, not made. We hear comments implying this from both teachers and parents. They seem to believe that good teaching happens if the teacher has a knack with children and keeps them reasonably attentive and enthusiastic about learning. It is commonly accepted in many colleges of education that teaching is an art that cannot be taught.

Perhaps because of this belief, students emerge from American colleges of education with little training in how to design and teach effective lessons. It is assumed that teachers will discover this for themselves. Courses in teaching methods are designed to serve a different purpose. On the one hand, they present theories of learning and cognitive development. Although these enable students to quote the major theorists currently in vogue, the theories remain broad generalizations that are difficult to apply to everyday tasks in the classroom. At the opposite extreme, these methods courses provide specific suggestions for activities and materials that are easy to use and that children should enjoy (for example, the fact that Cheerios make handy counters for teaching basic number facts). Beginning teachers are given information that is

157

either too general to be applied readily or so specific that it has only limited usefulness. Experienced American teachers complain that most of what they know had to be learned by themselves, alone, on the job.[1]

Curiously, we deny our teachers the apprenticeships that are commonly accepted as effective means for training other professionals. The training grounds for American teachers are large college classes and then the classrooms in which they spend only a few months as student teachers. None of us would allow ourselves to be treated by a doctor who had not spent several years working in a hospital under the supervision of experienced physicians. Yet we are willing to subject our children to teachers who, after completing their coursework, have had only a brief period of student teaching, often under the supervision of a practicing teacher who is so busy that she has neither the time nor the energy to give careful, critical attention to training a beginner. Teacher training in the United States is "sink-or-swim," a model that demands that beginning teachers perform the full complement of teaching duties from the first day they are on the job.[2]

Strategies for Training

The training of teachers in the United States takes place almost entirely in colleges and universities. This is evident in the number of years American elementary school teachers spend in formal education—more than eighteen for the Americans we interviewed, compared to about fifteen for teachers in Sendai and Taipei. Some American teachers had master's degrees; none of the Asian teachers had received more than a bachelor's degree. In fact, some of the teachers in China had no more than a high school education, and many of the teachers in Taiwan had only five years of schooling after graduating from lower middle school (grades seven to nine).

Asian teachers generally have fewer years of formal education than American teachers because Asian societies do not expect that the training of teachers will occur primarily in universities. The focus of their education is different as well. Asian teachers-to-be are more likely than Americans to major in liberal arts and to take courses in the substantive disciplines—for instance, mathematics or literature—rather than in methods for teaching these subjects. American teachers-in-training generally major in education, and take many courses in teaching methods. In our interviews, teachers in the United States reported they had taken an average of 4.8 college courses in methods for teaching reading and mathematics. (It is hard to evaluate the number of courses taken in Taiwan and Japan because they are not equivalent to those in the United States and also because some of the teachers did not attend college.)

The real training of Asian teachers occurs in their on-the-job experience *after* graduation from college. This experience has never been a major component in the training of American teachers. In Asia, graduates of teacher training programs are still considered novices who need the guidance and support of their experienced colleagues. In the United States, training comes to a near halt after the teachers acquire their teaching certificates. American teachers may take additional coursework in the evenings or during summer vacations, or they may attend district- or city-wide workshops from time to time. But these opportunities are not considered an essential part of the American system of teacher training.

In Japan, the system of teacher training is much like an apprenticeship. There is a systematic effort to pass on the accumulated wisdom of teaching practice to each new generation of teachers and to keep perfecting that kind of practice by providing for the continuing professional interaction of teachers. The teacher's first year of employment marks the beginning of a lengthy and elaborate process. By Japanese law, beginning teachers must receive a minimum of twenty days of in-service training during their first year on the job. Supervising this training are master teachers, selected for their teaching ability and their willingness to assist their young colleagues. During one-year leaves of absence from their own classrooms, they spend their days observing beginning teachers, offering suggestions for improvement, and counseling them about effective teaching techniques.

In addition, Japanese teachers, beginners as well as seasoned teachers, are required to perfect their teaching skills through interaction with other teachers. For instance, meetings are organized by the vice-principal and head teachers at their school. These experienced professionals assume responsibility for advising and guiding their young colleagues. The head teachers also organize meetings to discuss teaching techniques and to devise lesson plans and handouts. These discussions are very pragmatic and are aimed both at developing better teaching techniques and at constructing plans for specific lessons. A whole meeting might be devoted to the most effective ways to phrase questions about a topic or the most absorbing ways of capturing children's interest in a lesson. Meetings at each school are supplemented by informal district-wide study groups and by courses at municipal or prefectural education centers.[3]

A glimpse of what takes place in these study groups is provided in a conversation we recently had with a Japanese teacher. She and her colleagues spend a good deal of their time together working on lesson plans. After they finish a plan, one teacher from the group teaches the lesson to her students while the other teachers look on. Afterward, the group meets again to evaluate the teacher's performance and to make suggestions for improvement. In her school, there is an annual "teaching fair." Teachers from other schools are invited to visit the school and observe the lessons being taught. The visitors rate the lessons, and the teacher with the best lesson is declared the winner.

Opportunities to learn from other teachers are influenced, in part, by the physical arrangements of the schools. In Japanese and Chinese schools, a large room in each school is designed as a teachers' room, and each teacher is assigned a desk in this room. Here they spend their time away from the classroom preparing lessons, correcting students' papers, and discussing teaching techniques. American teachers, isolated in their own classrooms, find it much harder to discuss their work with colleagues. Their desks and teaching materials are in their own classrooms, and the only common space available to teachers is usually a cramped room that often houses supplies and the school's duplicating facilities, along with a few chairs and a coffee machine. Rarely do teachers have enough time in their visits to the "teachers' lounge" to engage in serious discussions of educational policy or teaching practices.

Effects of a Common Curriculum

Teachers find it easier to share helpful tips and techniques among themselves when they are all teaching the same lesson at about the same time. Teaching is also easier if they have access to materials of high quality. Publishers and manufacturers are willing to invest more resources in the production of classroom materials when they know that there is the potential of a national market. In Japan, nearly all teachers require children to purchase a "math set," a box of colorful, well-designed materials used for illustrating and teaching basic mathematical concepts. Workbooks, teachers' guides, and teaching aids sell well because they are directly relevant to what is being taught in classrooms. National television in Japan presents programs that show how master teachers handle particular lessons or concepts. In Taiwan, such demonstrations are available on sets of videotapes that cover the whole curriculum. In the United States, the curriculum may not be consistent within a city or even within a single school. As a result, American teachers have less incentive than Asian teachers to share experiences with one another or to benefit from the successes and failures that others have had in teaching particular lessons.

TEACHING: THE JOB

Competition for teaching jobs is far greater in Asia than in the United States. In Japan, about two-hundred thousand people take the difficult prefectural certification exams each year, but only about one fifth actually obtain teaching positions. The desirability of the teaching profession for Japanese students is evident in the fact that candidates who fail on their first attempt commonly make repeated efforts to pass the exams. In the United States, by contrast, certified teachers can almost certainly find a job if they are willing to relocate.

In Japan, the pay and the prestige of teaching relative to other professions are considerably above that found in the United States. Teachers' salaries in Japan are 2.4 times the national per capita income, as opposed to only 1.7 times for teachers in the United States. In addition, the ratio of Japanese teachers' salaries to the average salaries of various other occupations has been shown in every comparison to be higher than it is in the United States.[4] Young Japanese choose teaching without having to worry that they will suffer financially from their decision. Teachers and university professors in Japan make approximately equal salaries and enjoy nearly equivalent prestige. In the United States, the salary of an elementary school teacher may be only one third that of a college professor with comparable years of experience. The difference in status is symbolized, too, in the terms used for these positions. *Sensei,* the word for teacher in Japanese, is a term of respect and deference for those who teach first-graders as well as those who teach university students—an interesting contrast to the differential in status implied in the terms *teacher* and *professor* as they are used in the United States.

The Cost of Independence

Teachers in the United States greatly emphasize their independence, which often comes at the price of feelings of loneliness and isolation from other adults. Their closed classroom doors signal that they are in charge, and they cherish the authority they have over their schedule, curriculum, and classroom management. At the same time, the closed doors form barriers to communication, cutting teachers off from their colleagues. Teachers feel isolated, not only from one another, but also from parents. Rather than being able to welcome parents as partners in the education of children, they often encounter parents who pull back, leaving the teacher independent, but alone.

Adding further to the sense of isolation is the fact that American teachers, unlike other professionals, do not share a common body of knowledge and experience. The courses offered at different universities and colleges vary, and even among their required courses, there is often little common content from college to college. Student teaching, the only other activity in which all budding teachers participate, is a solitary endeavor shared only with the regular classroom teacher and perhaps a few fellow student teachers.

Schedule

The full realization of how little time American teachers have for interacting with other teachers became clear to us during a meeting in Beijing. We were discussing the teachers' workday. When we informed the Chinese teachers that American elementary school teachers are responsible for their classes all day long, with only an hour or less outside the classroom each day, they looked incredulous. How could any teacher be expected to do a good job when there is no time outside of class to prepare and correct lessons, work with individual children, consult with other teachers, and attend to all the matters that arise in a typical day

163

at school! Beijing teachers teach no more than three hours a day, unless the teacher is a homeroom teacher, in which case the total is four hours. During the first three grades the teaching assignment includes both reading and mathematics; for the upper three grades of elementary school, teachers specialize in one of these subjects. They spend the rest of their day at school carrying out all their other responsibilities to their students and to the school. The situation is similar in Japan. According to our estimate, Japanese elementary school teachers are in charge of classes only 60 percent of the time they are at school. In fact, Japanese law limits the amount of time a teacher may spend in front of a classroom to twenty-three hours for a six-day week—no more than four hours a day.[5]

Large amounts of nonteaching time at school are available to Asian teachers for two reasons. The first is the larger class size. By having more students in each class but the same number of teachers in the school, all teachers can have a lower teaching load. Time is freed up for teachers to meet and work together on a daily basis, to prepare lessons for the next day, to work with individual children, and to attend staff meetings. Although class sizes are large, the overall ratio of students to teachers within a school does not differ greatly from that in the United States.

The second factor increasing the time available to Japanese and Chinese teachers is the greater number of hours they spend at school each day. Teachers in Sendai, Beijing, and Taipei spent an average of 9.5, 9.7, and 9.1 hours per day, respectively, compared to only 7.3 hours for the American teachers. Asian teachers arrive at school early and stay late, which gives them time to meet together and to work with children who need extra help. Most American teachers, in contrast, arrive at school shortly before classes begin and leave not long after they end. This does not necessarily result in a shorter work week for American teachers. What it does mean is that they must devote their evenings and weekends to schoolwork.

Professional Life

Certain attributes differentiate the life of a professional from that of other workers. Professionals have longer and more specialized training, greater freedom to organize their time, greater personal responsibility for directing their own work, and the respect that comes from the uniqueness and quality of their contributions. But, other than bearing the responsibility for their own teaching, American teachers share few of these attributes. And they share little of the respect that at least some teachers once enjoyed in this country. For example, a teacher in a junior high school in Brooklyn voiced a complaint shared by many teachers in a recent piece published in *The New York Times:*

> Critics are missing the point when they equate teachers with "other city workers." Teachers are college educated. They perform a rare and special function in society. Is it fair to equate us with garbage collectors, clerks and transit workers?[6]

Such a plea by teachers in Taiwan and Japan is inconceivable. There is no question that teachers are professionals. Although in China these days teachers may suffer the kinds of inequities in salary that other Chinese intellectuals face, they still retain their admired professional status.

Another frequent complaint of American teachers is the burnout they feel after teaching the same subjects at the same grade level at the same school year after year. This is less often a problem with Asian teachers, whose professional lives allow greater opportunities for personal development. For example, elementary school teachers in Japan are responsible for one group of children for two, and sometimes three, years. This means that they rarely teach at the same grade level for two years in a row. In addition, teachers rotate periodically through all six grades of elementary school and, every three to seven years, from school to school within the city.

These practices expose teachers to new challenges and new ideas, new colleagues and supervisors, and new sets of parents. Adding to their motivation are the opportunities for advancement that result from the practice of appointing school administrators from among the ranks of teachers. Principals, assistant principals, and head teachers all start out in Japan as classroom teachers. A prime qualification for their supervisory position is their own success as teachers, not coursework in educational administration—the route to an administrative position in the United States.

DEFINING THE IDEAL TEACHER

American teachers and the American public hold a notion of the ideal teacher that is very different from that held in Asia. This is evident in the responses teachers in Beijing and Chicago gave when we asked them about the attributes most important for a good teacher to have. We listed five: ability to explain things clearly, sensitivity to the needs and personality characteristics of individual children, enthusiasm about teaching, having high standards for children, and patience. We then asked the teachers to select the one that they believed to be the most important; the results are shown in Figure 8.1.

The attributes chosen more often by the American than by the Chinese teachers were sensitivity and patience. These choices are in line with the American emphasis on individual differences and the high priority on building children's self-esteem. For the Chinese teachers, sensitivity and patience were chosen by fewer than 10 percent of the teachers. Their most frequent emphasis was on factors more directly relevant to the process of teaching subject matter: the ability to explain things clearly and to be enthusiastic. Fewer than 10 percent of the American teachers chose clarity of explanation, a strong indication of their lack of emphasis on academic instruction as the teacher's primary task.

In Asia, the ideal teacher is a skilled performer. As with the

FIGURE 8.1
Teachers' judgments about the most important attributes
required to be a good teacher.

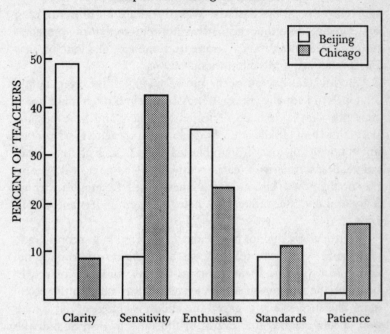

actor or musician, the substance of the curriculum becomes the script or the score; the goal is to perform the role or piece as effectively and creatively as possible. Rather than executing the curriculum as a mere routine, the skilled teacher strives to perfect the presentation of each lesson. She uses the teaching techniques she has learned and imposes her own interpretation on these techniques in a manner that she thinks will interest and motivate her pupils.

In America, teachers are judged to be successful when they are innovative, inventive, and original. Skilled presentation of a standard lesson is not sufficient and may even be disparaged as indicating a lack of innovative talent. It is as if American teachers

167

were expected to write their own play or create their own concerto day after day and then perform it with expertise and finesse. These two models, the skilled performer and the innovator, have very different value in the East and West. It is hard for us in the West to appreciate that innovation does not require that the presentation be totally new, but can come from thoughtful additions, new interpretations, and skillful modifications.

Good teaching requires the use of examples; however, not all examples are equally effective. In Asia, teachers often make use of examples that have been perfected by others and have become part of the lore of skilled teaching. American teachers feel conflict about borrowing ideas from other teachers. In seeking to be innovative, many American teachers attempt to come up with examples on their own. Unfortunately, these untried examples often go awry and confuse, rather than help, children understand a concept.

A particularly memorable instance occurred in a second-grade classroom, where the teacher was attempting to introduce the concept of average. In an effort to tap her students' interest in baseball, the teacher began the lesson by discussing batting averages. She successfully engaged the children's interest, but it took only a few seconds for several of the boys to discern that the teacher was unaware of the intricacies of baseball statistics. When she realized this, she quickly abandoned the example. Even if she had understood how to compute a batting average, she would have had great difficulty relating the example to what she was trying to teach. The idiosyncratic use of the term "average" in baseball bears little relevance to the procedure for computing a mean, in this case adding up five numbers and dividing by five.

PROBLEM CHILDREN

It would seem to go without saying that the main task of teachers is educating students in the content of the curriculum. Nevertheless, American teachers quickly explain that among other things, society expects them to function as counselors, clinical psychologists, and disciplinarians, to deal with children who have serious personal problems and who have lacked discipline at home. These multiple demands exhaust even the most energetic teachers.

"How would you handle this one?" one American teacher challenged us. "One of the girls in my class came up today and said that her mother had told her that morning that she was putting her up for adoption. The girl was crying, and of course she was very upset. She looked at me as if I could do something to help solve her problem. What can I do? How can I help her? How am I going to shake the feeling that I should be doing something? How can I expect her to learn anything in my class from now on?"

This is not an isolated example; week after week, American teachers must cope with children who present them with complex, wrenching personal problems. In a recent book, Tracy Kidder chronicles a year in the life of Chris Zajac, a fifth-grade teacher.[7] What is most disheartening is the degree to which teaching became a secondary issue in Ms. Zajac's life. She did not have time to think about which technique would work best for teaching a particular concept. Instead, she spent her days and nights worrying about Clarence, whose discipline problems disrupted the entire classroom; about Jimmy, who stayed up nights watching movies on TV and could not keep his eyes open in class; and about the other troubled children she encountered every day in her class.

What Ms. Zajac and other teachers are telling us is that the lives of many children in their classes are such a mess that they cannot function well at school. It is not uncommon to hear teachers despair of what they can accomplish. The pessimistic feeling of many teachers is evident in the list of problems mentioned by one of the American teachers we interviewed:

> One-parent families, mothers who work and have no time, children who must go to some kind of care center after school hours

169

to wait for their mothers; some children have a house key and go home to an empty house before the parent arrives home. Students have so many personal and family problems that they can barely cope.

How can teachers, under such circumstances, get down to the business of teaching? How can we control conditions in the classroom so that children can concentrate on what they are supposed to be learning? We asked first-grade teachers in Beijing and Chicago to estimate the percentage of children who would be likely to display various behavior problems during their early days at school. Fewer Chinese than American children were considered to be disorganized, to have trouble following directions, or to display nervousness in class. Their teachers saw Chinese children as less fidgety and inattentive, and less likely to complain of fatigue, stomachaches, and headaches. These problems go beyond the resources of teachers and schools; they can be improved only at the level of the family and society.

Imposing Discipline

Imposing discipline demands a great deal of energy. Whether American children are especially difficult to manage or their own disciplinary techniques are inadequate, American teachers devote much more time to discipline than do their Asian peers.

One index of the need for discipline is the degree to which American children engage in irrelevant activities in the classroom, as we described in Chapter 7. Such activities as talking to other children and wandering about the classroom diminish the child's own opportunities for learning and are potentially disruptive to other children. This type of irrelevant behavior, in addition to the fidgeting and inattentiveness often described by American teachers, makes maintaining discipline a pervasive and difficult problem in American classrooms.

Techniques employed to ensure discipline in American classrooms typically are teacher-centered. It is the teacher who quiets the class, who tries to control rowdiness, and who scolds the errant child. Chinese and Japanese rely on the children themselves for maintaining discipline. Consider the following scene, which we observed in a Japanese first-grade classroom. The teacher tried to begin the daily mathematics lesson. The children were noisy and continued their loud conversations. The teacher paused, looked at the class, and then called on the child who was the day's classroom leader: "The children are too noisy. Until they are quiet, I cannot teach," she said matter-of-factly. The young leader went into action. She stood, faced the class, and announced, "Please stand up. We are so noisy, teacher can't teach." The children quickly became quiet. The leader turned to the teacher and reported: "We are quiet now." The children bowed to their teacher and sat down, attentive as the teacher announced, "We will begin."

In addition to relying on children, Asian teachers can usually count on the full cooperation of parents. American parents are less supportive of teachers' efforts to discipline their children and at times may even hold the teacher responsible for a child's errant behavior. They may take the child's side and criticize the teacher either directly or to the principal. When there is a lack of cooperation and mutual respect between parent and teacher, children may slyly play off one against the other and, in the conflict, undermine the teacher's authority. When disagreements arise between parents and teachers, American parents, rather than working with the teacher to resolve the difficulty, would be likely to try to have their children transferred to another classroom—a solution that could never occur in a Japanese school.

DEFINING THE PROBLEM

It is easy to blame teachers for the problems confronting American education, as the American public is prone to do. The accusation is unfair. We do not provide teachers adequate training and

171

yet we expect that on their own they will become innovative teachers; we cast them in the roles of surrogate parents, counselors, and psychotherapists, and still expect them to be effective teachers; and we keep them so busy in the classroom that they have little time or opportunity for professional development once they have joined the teaching profession. We require teachers to spend nearly all their time in charge of children and give them little time to reflect on the practices of teaching. Being an elementary school teacher in the United States at the end of the twentieth century is extraordinarily difficult, and the demands made by American society exhaust even the most energetic among them. "I'm dancing as fast as I can," is the way one teacher summarized her feelings about her job, "but with all the things that I'm supposed to do, I just can't keep up."

Americans are not convinced that teaching should be one of our most esteemed professions. They are unwilling to spend the funds for training teachers that they readily apply to the training of other professionals. Nor do they consider that their children's teacher merits the same respect and compensation that they are willing to bestow on their doctor or lawyer. It is true that Americans attracted to teaching are not among the most able students in our colleges and universities; in fact, year after year, reports of college entrance scores reveal that the lowest average scores are obtained by students in colleges of education. Given the current status of the teaching profession, how can we break out of this self-defeating cycle? How can we hope to attract outstanding students to the profession and endow it with the respect it deserves?

Critics argue that problems facing the American teacher are unique, and that it is futile to consider what Japanese and Chinese teachers are like in seeking solutions to educational problems in the United States. One of the frequent arguments is that the students in the typical Asian classroom share a common language and culture, are well disciplined and attentive, and are not distracted by family crises and their own personal problems, whereas the typical American teacher is burdened with a diverse and distracted group of students. To be sure, the conditions encountered by teachers differ greatly among these societies, but much of what gives American classrooms their aura of disarray and disorganization may be traced, at least in part, to how schools are organized and teachers are trained.

Efforts to prepare teachers for their jobs are undermined by those who believe that teaching is an art, the expression of an ability with which some people are endowed and others are not. We need a system that gives teachers opportunities to learn from one another and to benefit from the accumulated wisdom of generations of skilled practitioners. We cannot cast teachers out on their own after only a single term of practice teaching and then be surprised at their shortcomings. Many Chinese and Japanese teachers have told us that the most important contributions to their professional development come from interaction with other teachers. Ironically, such interactions are what the American system of education has denied its teachers.

The reform of education in the United States requires a rethinking of the profession of teaching. No other change is as basic as this one for, after all, any effort to reform the structure or organization of education ultimately depends on the skill with which it is carried out by teachers.

Chapter 9

The Practice of Teaching

When the chimes of the public address system signal that class is about to begin, Chinese and Japanese children drift toward their desks. The teacher stands in front of the class as a cue that the lesson will soon start. The room quiets. "Let us begin," says the teacher in Sendai. After brief reciprocal bows between pupils and teacher, the teacher opens the class with a description of what will be accomplished during the class period. From that point until the teacher summarizes the day's lesson and announces, "We are through," the Japanese elementary school class—like those in Taiwan and China—consists of teacher and students working together toward the goals described at the beginning of the class.

Contrast this scene with a fifth-grade American mathematics classroom that we recently visited. Immediately after getting the students' attention, the teacher pointed out that today was Tuesday, "band day," and that all students in the band should go to the band room. "Those of you doing the news report today should meet over there in the corner," he continued. He then began the mathematics class with the remaining students by reviewing the solution to a computation problem that had been included in the previous day's homework. After this brief review, the teacher directed the students' attention to the blackboard, where the day's assignment had been written. The teacher then spent most of the rest of the period walking about the room monitoring the children's work, talking to individual children about questions or errors, and uttering "shush" whenever the students began talking among themselves.

This example is typical of the American classrooms we described in Chapter 7, classrooms where, compared to their Asian peers, students spend more time in transition and less in academic activities, more time working on their own and less being instructed by the teacher; where teachers spend much of their time working with individual students and attending to matters of discipline.

The focus of this chapter is the process of teaching in American and Asian classrooms. We seek to clarify principles followed by the teachers in the different cultures. We focus on mathematics classes rather than on subjects such as reading, where cultural differences in teaching practices may be more strongly determined by differences in the content of what is being taught. It is likely that teaching how to multiply fractions transcends cultural differences, whereas teaching children how to read Chinese characters may require different approaches from those used to teach children to read English.

OBSERVING IN CLASSROOMS

One frequently sees reports on television and in books and newspapers purporting to depict what happens inside Japanese and Chinese classrooms. These reports usually are based on impressions gathered during brief visits to classrooms—most likely classrooms that the visitor's contact in Asia has pre-selected. As a result, it is difficult to gauge the generality of what was seen and reported. Without observing large, representative samples of schools and teachers, it is impossible to analyze the teaching practices of any culture.

The descriptions that we present are based on two large observational studies of first- and fifth-grade classrooms that we conducted in Japan, Taiwan, China, and the United States. In contrast to informal observations, the strength of formal studies such as ours is that the observations are made according to consistent rules about where, when, who, and what to observe.

In the previous chapter we discussed some of the results of our first observational study, in which we observed 120 classrooms for 20 hours each in Sendai, Taipei, and Minneapolis. Our second study took place in 204 classrooms, 40 classrooms each in Sendai and Taipei, 44 in Beijing, and 80 in Chicago. Observers visited each classroom four times over a one- to two-week period, yielding a total of 800 hours of observations. The observers, who were residents of the city in which they observed, wrote down as much as they could about what transpired during each mathematics class. Tape recordings made during the classes assisted the observers in filling in any missing information. These detailed narrative accounts yielded even richer information than we obtained in the first study, where the observers followed predefined categories for coding behavior during their observations.

After the narrative records had been translated into English, we divided each observation into segments, which we defined as beginning each time there was a change in topic, materials, or activity. For example, a segment began when students put away their textbooks and began working on a worksheet, or when the teacher stopped lecturing and asked some of the students to write their solutions to a problem on the blackboard.

If we were asked briefly to characterize classes in Japan and China, we would say that they consist of coherent lessons that are presented in a thoughtful, relaxed, and nonauthoritarian manner. Teachers frequently involve students as sources of information.

Lessons are oriented toward problem-solving rather than rote mastery of facts and procedures, and make use of many different types of representational materials. The role assumed by the teacher is that of knowledgeable guide, rather than that of prime dispenser of information and arbiter of what is correct. There is frequent verbal interaction in the classroom as the teacher attempts to stimulate students to produce, explain, and evaluate solutions to problems. These characteristics contradict stereotypes held by most Westerners about Asian teaching practices. Lessons are not rote; they are not filled with drill. Teachers do not spend large amounts of time lecturing to children; and the children are not passive automatons but active participants in the learning process.

COHERENCE

One way to think of a lesson is by using the analogy of a story. A good story is highly organized; it has a beginning, a middle, and an end, and it follows a protagonist who meets challenges and resolves problems that arise along the way. Above all, a good story engages the reader's interest in a series of interconnected events, each of which is best understood in the context of the events that precede and follow it.

In Asia, instruction is guided by this concept of a lesson. The curricula include coherent lessons, each carefully designed to fill a forty- to fifty-minute class period with sustained attention to the development of some concept or skill. Like a good story, the lesson has an introduction, a conclusion, and a consistent theme.

We can illustrate what we are talking about with this account of a fifth-grade mathematics class we observed in Japan:

> The teacher walks in carrying a large paper bag full of clinking glass. Her entry into the classroom with a large paper bag is highly unusual, and by the time she has placed it on her desk, the students

177

are regarding her with rapt attention. What's in the bag? She begins to pull out items, placing them one by one on her desk. She removes a pitcher and a vase. A beer bottle evokes laughter and surprise. She soon has six containers lined up on her desk. The children continue to watch intently, glancing back and forth at each other as they seek to understand the purpose of this display.

The teacher, looking thoughtfully at the containers, poses a question: "I wonder which one would hold the most water?" Hands go up, and the teacher calls on different students to give their guesses: "the pitcher," "the beer bottle," "the teapot." The teacher stands aside and ponders: "Some of you said one thing, others said something different. You don't agree with one another. There must be some way we can find out who is correct. How can we know who is correct?" Interest is high, and the discussion continues.

The students soon agree that to find out how much each container holds, they will need to fill the containers with something. How about water? The teacher finds some buckets and sends several children out to fill them with water. When they return, the teacher says: "Now what do we do?" Again there is a discussion, and after several minutes the children decide that they will need to use a smaller container to measure how much water fits into each of the larger containers. They decide on a drinking cup, and one of the students warns that they all have to fill each cup to the same level—otherwise the measure won't be the same for all the groups.

At this point the teacher divides the class into their groups *(han)*, and gives each group one of the containers and a drinking cup. Each group fills its container, counts how many cups of water it holds, and writes the result in a notebook. When all the groups have completed the task, the teacher calls on the leader of each group to report on its findings, and notes the results on the blackboard. She has written the names of the containers in a column on the left and a scale from 1 to 6 along the bottom. As each group makes its report, the teacher draws a bar representing the amount the container holds: pitcher, 4.5 cups; vase, 3 cups; beer bottle, 1.5 cups; and so on.

Finally the teacher returns to the question she posed at the beginning of the lesson: Which container holds the most water? She reviews how they were able to solve the problem, and points out that the answer is now contained in the bar graph on the board. She then arranges the containers on the table according to how much they hold, and writes a rank order on each container, from 1 to 6. She ends the class with a brief review of what they have done. No definitions of ordinate and abscissa, no discussion of how to make a graph preceded the example—these all became obvious in the course of the lesson, and only at the end did the teacher mention the terms that describe the horizontal and vertical axes of the graph they had made.

We begin to see how Asian teachers create coherent lessons. The lessons almost always begin with a practical problem such as the example we have just given or with a word problem written on the blackboard. Asian teachers, to a much greater degree than American teachers, give coherence to their lessons by introducing the lesson with a word problem (see Figure 9.1). It is not uncommon for an Asian teacher to organize an entire lesson around the solution of a single problem. The teacher leads the children to recognize what is known and what is unknown, and directs the students' attention to the critical parts of the problem. Teachers attempt to see that all the children understand the problem, and even mechanics, such as mathematical computation, are presented in the context of solving a problem.

Before ending the lesson, the teacher reviews what has been learned and relates it to the problem she posed at the beginning of the lesson. American teachers are much less likely than Asian teachers to begin and end lessons in this way. For example, we found that fifth-grade teachers in Beijing spent eight times as long at the end of the class period summarizing the lessons as did those in Chicago.

FIGURE 9.1

Percent of lessons in which the teacher was observed to present students with a written or oral real-world problem.

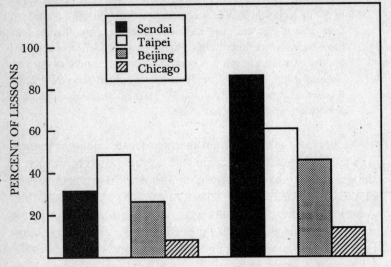

Threats to Coherence

Even when a lesson is designed to be coherent, it is not necessarily perceived that way by the students. Take, for example, the following description of an American first-grade lesson on measurement:

> The teacher begins by having children compare pairs of various objects to determine which of each pair is longer—a pencil versus a crayon, a paper clip versus a piece of chalk, and so on. She calls on the children to report the results of their comparisons.
>
> After several minutes of discussion the teacher says: "Okay, take out your workbooks and open them to page twelve. Look at the first line, where there is a picture of a pencil. I want you to measure your desk in pencils. Find out how many pencils it takes to go

across your desk. Now write the answer on the first line in your workbook." After the children carry out these instructions, the teacher continues: "On the next line there is a picture of a green crayon. We don't have any green crayons so we are going to use blue crayons." At this point, the teacher interrupts the lesson to pass out blue crayons. She then continues: "Now write the number of blue crayons next to the line that has a picture of a green crayon."

After the students complete the same exercise using several more objects, the teacher says: "Now take out your centimeter ruler and measure the number of centimeters across your desk and write the number on the line in your workbooks." By the time the children complete this task, the teacher decides that it is time to move on to the reading lesson. Without further comment, she tells the children to put away their workbooks and take out their reading books.

This sequence of activities had all the elements necessary for creating a coherent lesson, but it seems unlikely that the children perceived its coherence, or even its meaning, without the teacher's helping them to relate the different parts of the lesson to one another. By failing to explain the purpose or the interrelation of the various activities, the lesson devolved into three unconnected exercises: comparing objects, measuring the desk with the objects, and then measuring the desk with a standard measure. It is doubtful that many children understood the relations among the activities: that when it is not possible to compare lengths directly, it becomes necessary to use some unit, and that comparability of measurement across diverse times and places requires the use of a standard unit. Coherence is lost because of the teacher's failure to interrelate the components of the lesson. But there are also other common threats to coherence.

Irrelevant interruptions often add to children's difficulty in perceiving lessons as a coherent whole. In our American observations, the teacher interrupted the flow of the lesson with irrelevant comments or the class was interrupted by someone else in 20 percent of all first-grade lessons and 47 percent of all fifth-grade lessons. In Sendai, Taipei, and Beijing interruptions occurred less than 10 percent of the time at both grade levels. In fact, no interruptions of either type were recorded during the eighty hours of observation in Beijing fifth-grade classrooms. In contrast, the mathematics lesson in one of the American classrooms we visited was interrupted every morning by a woman from the cafeteria who polled the children about their lunch plans and collected money from those who planned to eat the hot lunch.

Coherence is also disrupted by frequent shifting from one topic to another within a single lesson. This was evident in many American lessons we observed. The teacher might begin with a segment on measurement, then proceed to a segment on simple addition, then to a segment on telling time, and then to a second segment on addition. These segments constitute a math class, but they are hardly a coherent lesson. Twenty-one percent of the shifts within American lessons were to different topics (rather than to different materials or activities), compared with only 5 percent in the Japanese lessons.

The American teachers' tendency to shift topics so frequently may be due to their desire to capitalize on variety as a means of capturing children's interest. Asian teachers also seek variety, but they tend to introduce new activities instead of new topics. Shifts in materials—for example, from working with numerals to working with concrete objects—do not necessarily pose a threat to coherence as long as both are used to represent the same subtraction problem. Shifting the topic, on the other hand, risks destroying the coherence of the lesson.

Coherence is also threatened by prolonged seatwork. When children must work alone for long periods of time without guidance or reaction from the teacher, they begin to lose focus on the purpose of their activity. Asian teachers, as we have discussed, assign less seatwork than American teachers; furthermore, they use seatwork differently. Asian teachers tend to use short, frequent periods of seatwork, alternating between discussing problems and allowing children to work problems on their own. When seatwork is embedded within the lesson, instruction and practice are tightly interwoven into a coherent whole. Teachers can gauge children's understanding of the preceding part of the lesson by observing how they solve the practice problems. Interspersing seatwork with instruction in this way helps the teacher assess how rapidly she can proceed through the lesson.

American teachers, on the other hand, tend to relegate seatwork to one long period at the end of the class, where it becomes little more than a time for repetitious practice. In Chicago, 59 percent of all fifth-grade lessons ended with a period of seatwork, compared with 23 percent in Sendai and 14 percent in Taipei. American teachers often do not discuss the work or its connection to the goal of the lesson, or publicly evaluate its accuracy. Seatwork was never evaluated or discussed during 48 percent of all American fifth-grade lessons observed, compared to less than 3 percent of Japanese classes and 6 percent of Taiwan classes. Can seatwork be an effective means of learning when it is completed in a ·nonresponsive setting?

USES OF WORDS AND OBJECTS

The goal of elementary school mathematics is often defined as acquiring familiarity with mathematical symbols and their manipulation; for example, children must learn the place-value system of numeration and how to manipulate numerals to add, subtract, multiply, and divide. In addition, children are expected to understand the meaning of these symbols and to be able to apply them to solving problems. In order to accomplish these goals, teachers rely primarily on two powerful tools for representing mathematics: language and concrete objects. How effectively teachers use them is critical in determining how well children will understand mathematics.

Language in the Mathematics Classroom

One common function of language in mathematics is to define terms and state rules for performing mathematical operations. A second, broader function is to use language as a means of integrating what children know about mathematics and of connecting mathematical operations to the real world. We find that American elementary school teachers are more prone to use language to define terms and state rules than are Asian teachers, who, in their efforts to make mathematics meaningful, use language as a means of clarification and elaboration.

Here is an example of what we mean by defining terms and stating rules:

> An American teacher announces that the lesson today concerns fractions. She writes the fraction 1/2 on the blackboard and uses it to define what is meant by a fraction in terms of its parts. She describes how the 2 represents the total number of parts and the 1 indicates the number of parts represented in this fraction. She then defines the numerator and the denominator, and checks to see if the children remember these names. "What do we call this?" she asks. "And this?" After assuring herself that the children understand the meaning of the terms, she has the children represent various quantities using fractional notation.

Asian teachers tend to reverse the procedure. They focus initially on interpreting and defining a problem and then on discussing the ways the problem can be represented through mathematical notation. Only later, when children have had experience with fractions, does the teacher define terms and state rules. In the following example, a third-grade teacher in Japan was teaching a lesson that introduced the notation system for fractions:

> The lesson began with the teacher posing the question of how many liters of juice (colored water) were contained in a large beaker. "More than one liter," answered one child. "One and a

half liters," answered another. After several children had made guesses, the teacher suggested that they pour the juice into some one-liter beakers and see. Horizontal lines on each beaker divided it into thirds. The juice filled one beaker and part of a second. The teacher pointed out that the juice came up to the first line on the second beaker—only one of the three parts was full. The procedure was repeated with a second set of beakers to illustrate the concept of one half. After stating that there had been one and one-out-of-three parts of a liter of juice in the first big beaker and one and one-out-of-two parts of a liter in the second, the teacher wrote the fractions on the board. He continued the lesson by asking the children how to represent two parts out of three, two parts out of five, and so forth. Near the end of the period he mentioned the term fraction for the first time and attached names to the numerator and the denominator. He ended the lesson by summarizing how fractions can be used to represent the parts of a whole.

In the second example, the concept of fractions emerged from a meaningful experience; in the first, it was introduced initially as an abstract concept. The terms and operations in the second example flowed naturally from the teacher's questions and discussion; in the first, language was used primarily for defining and summarizing rules. Mathematics ultimately requires abstract representation, but young children understand it more readily if it is embedded in a meaningful context than if it is presented as what seem to be arbitrary definitions and rules.

Asian teachers generally are more likely than American teachers to engage their students, even very young ones, in discussions of mathematical concepts. In one memorable example recorded by our observers, a Japanese first-grade teacher began her class by posing this question to one of her students: "Would you explain the difference between what we learned in yesterday's lesson and what you came across in preparing for today's lesson?" The young student thought for a long time, but then answered the question intelligently, explaining how a rectangle was related to a triangle.

Verbal discussion in American classrooms is more short-answer in nature—oriented, for example, toward clarifying the correct way to implement a computational procedure. Our observations confirm what is implicit in the examples we have presented. Asian teachers use more verbal explanations—which we defined as statements made by either students or the teacher that are more than one sentence in length—than do American teachers. For example, 47 percent of the segments in the Japanese observations, but only 20 percent of the segments in the American observations, contained such explanations.

Concrete Representations

Every elementary school student in Sendai possesses a "math set," a box of colorful, well-designed materials for teaching mathematical concepts: tiles, clock, ruler, checkerboard, colored triangles, beads, and many other attractive objects. In Taipei, every classroom is equipped with a similar but larger set of such objects. In Beijing, where there is much less money available for purchasing such materials, teachers improvise with colored paper, wax fruit, plates, and other easily obtained objects. In all cases, these concrete objects are considered to be critically important tools for teaching mathematics. It is through manipulating these objects and thinking about them that children can form important links between real-world problems and abstract mathematical notations.

American teachers are much less likely than Chinese or Japanese teachers to use concrete objects to represent mathematical ideas. At fifth grade, for example, Sendai teachers were nearly twice as likely to use concrete objects as the Chicago teachers, and Taipei teachers were nearly five times as likely. There is also a subtle but important difference in the way Asian and American teachers use concrete objects. Japanese teachers, for example, use the items in the math set repeatedly throughout the elementary school years, and introduce small tiles in a high percentage of first-grade lessons. American teachers seek variety. They may use Popsicle sticks in one lesson, and marbles, Cheerios, M&M's, checkers, poker chips, or plastic animals in another. The American view is that objects should be varied in order to maintain children's interest. The Asian view is that using a variety of representational materials may confuse children, and thereby make it more difficult for them to use the objects for the representation and solution of mathematics problems. Multiplication is easier to understand when the same tiles are used as were used when the children learned to add.

Through the skillful use of concrete objects, Asian teachers are able to teach elementary school children to understand and solve problems that are not introduced in American curricula until much later. An example occurred in a fourth-grade mathematics lesson we observed in Japan. The problem the teacher posed is a difficult one for fourth-graders, and its solution is generally not taught in the United States until students take a course in algebra. This is the problem:

> There is a total of thirty-eight children in Akira's class. There are six more boys than there are girls. How many boys and how many girls are in the class?

This lesson began with a discussion of the problem and with the children proposing ways to solve it. After the discussion, the teacher handed each child two strips of paper, one longer than the other, and told the class that the strips would be used to help them think about the problem. She asked the children to line up the strips next to each other and to decide which one represented the boys. "The longer one," responded one of the students, "because there are more boys." Another student pointed out that the amount the longer one protruded beyond the shorter represented how many more boys than girls there were in the class. The procedure for solving the problem then unfolded as the teacher, through skillful questioning, led the children to the solution: The number of girls was found by taking the total of both strips, subtracting 6 to make the strips of equal length, and then dividing by 2. The number of boys could be found, of course, by adding 6 to the number of girls. With this concrete visual representation of the problem and careful guidance from the teacher, even fourth-graders were able to understand the problem and its solution.

TEACHERS, STUDENTS, AND THE SOURCES OF KNOWLEDGE

A common Western stereotype is that of the Asian teacher as an authoritarian purveyor of information, one who expects students to listen and memorize correct answers or correct procedures rather than to construct knowledge themselves. This may be an accurate description of Asian high school teachers,[1] but, as we have seen in previous examples, it does not describe the dozens of elementary school teachers that we have observed.

Chinese and Japanese teachers rely on students to generate ideas and evaluate the correctness of the ideas (see Figure 9.2). The possibility that they will be called upon to state their own solution as well as to evaluate what another student has proposed keeps Asian students alert, but this technique has two other important functions. First, it engages students in the lesson, increasing their motivation by making them feel they are participants in a group process. Second, it conveys a more realistic impression of how knowledge is acquired. Mathematics, for example, is a body of knowledge that has evolved gradually through a process of argument and proof. Learning to argue about mathematical ideas is fundamental to understanding mathematics. Chinese and Japanese children begin learning these skills in the first grade; many American elementary school students are never exposed to them.

We can illustrate the way Asian teachers use students' ideas with the following example: A fifth-grade teacher in Taiwan began her mathematics lesson by calling attention to a six-sided

FIGURE 9.2

Percent of lessons in which the teacher was observed to use students' answers in discussion.

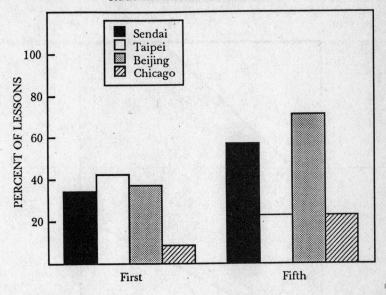

figure she had drawn on the blackboard (see Figure 9.3). She asked the students how they might go about finding the area of the shaded region. "I don't want you to tell me what the actual area is. Just tell me the approach you would use to solve the problem. Think of as many different ways as you can to determine the area that I have drawn in yellow chalk." She allowed the students several minutes to work in small groups, and then called upon a child from each group to describe the group's solution. After each proposal—many of which were quite complex—the teacher asked all students in the class whether the procedure described could yield a correct answer. After several different procedures had been suggested, the teacher moved on to a second problem, with a different embedded figure, and repeated the process. Neither teacher nor students actually carried out a solution to the problem

189

FIGURE 9.3

Think of as many ways as you can for determining the area of
the shaded region.

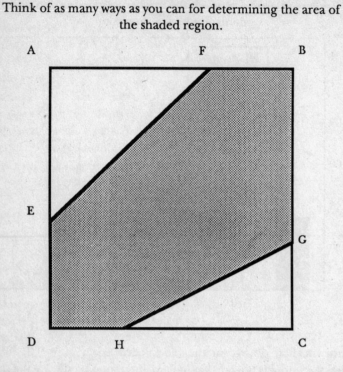

until all the alternative solutions had been discussed. The lesson
ended with the teacher affirming the importance of coming up
with multiple solutions. "After all," she said, "we face many problems every day in the real world. We have to remember that there
is not only one way we can solve each problem."

American teachers are less likely to give students opportunities
to respond at such length. Although a great deal of interaction
appears to occur in American classrooms—with teachers and
students posing questions and giving answers—American teachers
generally ask questions that are answerable with a yes or a no, or
with a short phrase. They seek a correct answer, and continue
calling on students until one produces it. "Since we can't subtract

eight from six," says an American teacher, "We have to . . .
what?" Hands go up. The teacher calls on a girl who says, "Borrow." "Correct," the teacher replies. This kind of interchange
does not establish the student as a valid source of information, for
the final arbiter of the correctness of the students' opinions is still
the teacher. The situation is very different in Asian classrooms,
where children are likely to be asked to explain their answers and
other children are then called upon to evaluate their correctness.

Clear evidence of these differing beliefs about the roles of students and teachers appears in the observations of how teachers
evaluate students' responses. The most frequent form of evaluation used by American teachers was praise, a technique that is
rarely used in either Taiwan or Japan.

Praise cuts off discussion, and highlights the teacher's role as the
authority. It also encourages children to be satisfied with their
performance rather than informing them about where they need
improvement. Chinese and Japanese teachers have a low tolerance for errors, and when they occur, they seldom ignore them.
Discussing errors helps to clarify misunderstandings, encourage
argument and justification, and involve students in the exciting
quest of assessing the strengths and weaknesses of the various
alternative solutions that have been proposed.

Why are American teachers often reluctant to encourage students to participate at greater length during mathematics lessons?
One possibility is that teachers feel insecure about the depth of
their own mathematical training. Placing more emphasis on students' explanations necessarily requires teachers to relinquish
some control over the direction the lesson will take. This can be
a frightening prospect to a teacher who is unprepared to evaluate
the validity of novel ideas that students inevitably propose.

USING ERRORS EFFECTIVELY

We have been struck by the different reactions of Asian and American teachers to children's errors. For Americans, errors tend to be interpreted as an indication of failure in learning the lesson. For Chinese and Japanese, they are an index of what still needs to be learned. As we indicated in Chapter 5, these divergent interpretations result in very different reactions—embarrassment on the part of the American children, relatively calm acceptance by Asian children. They also result in differences in the manner in which teachers make effective use of errors in their teaching.

We visited a fifth-grade classroom in Japan the first day the teacher introduced the problem of adding fractions with unequal denominators. The problem was simple: adding one third and one half. The children were told to solve the problem and that the class would then review the different solutions.

After everyone appeared to have completed the task, the teacher called on one of the students to give his answer and to explain his solution. "The answer is two fifths," he stated. Pointing first to the numerators and then to the denominators, he explained: "One plus one is two; three plus two is five. The answer is two fifths." Without comment, the teacher asked another boy for his solution. "Two point one plus three point one, when changed into a fraction, adds up to two fifths." The children in the classroom looked puzzled. The teacher, unperturbed, asked a third student for her solution. "The answer is five sixths." The student went on to explain how she had found the common denominator, changed the fractions so that each had this denominator, and then added them.

The teacher returned to the first solution. "How many of you think this solution is correct?" Most agreed that it was not. She used the opportunity to direct the children's attention to reasons why the solution was incorrect. "Which is larger, two fifths or one half?" The class agreed that it was one half. "It is strange, isn't it, that you could add a number to one half and get a number that is smaller than one half?" She went on to explain how the procedure the child used would result in the odd situation where, when one half was added to one half, the answer would be one half. In a similarly careful interactive manner, she discussed how the second boy had confused fractions with decimals to come up with his surprising answer. Rather than ignoring the incorrect solutions and concentrating her attention on the correct solution, the teacher capitalized on the errors the children made in order to dispel two common misconceptions about fractions.

We have not observed American teachers responding to children's errors so inventively. In one second-grade lesson we observed in which students were being taught subtraction with renaming, the teacher had several times given students examples that required borrowing. Each example followed the same pattern. In a problem like 23 minus 17, the teacher would ask a child, "Can we subtract 7 units from 3 units?" The child would promptly respond, "No." The teacher would then ask the whole class what should be done, to which the children, in unison, would respond, "Go borrow from our neighbor," referring to the tens column. In one of these interchanges the teacher posed the problem 34 minus 19, and asked a student if 9 units could be subtracted from 4 units. This time the pattern was broken: The student answered "Yes, it is minus 5." The teacher completely ignored what she considered to be the wrong answer, and simply asked her question again to another child. This time she got the answer she was looking for.

Perhaps because of the strong influence of behavioristic teaching, which says conditions should be arranged so that the learner avoids errors and makes only a reinforceable response, American teachers place little emphasis on the constructive use of errors as a teaching technique. Learning about what is wrong may hasten understanding of why the correct procedures are appropriate, but errors may also be interpreted as failure. And Americans, reluc-

tant to have such interpretations made of their children's performance, strive to avoid situations where this might happen.

TIME TO THINK

American elementary school students, watching a videotape of
a Japanese mathematics lesson, inevitably react to the pace: They
perceive unbearable slowness. The pace is slow, but the outcome
is impressive. Japanese teachers want their students to be reflective
and to gain a deep understanding of mathematics. Each concept
and skill is taught with great thoroughness, thereby eliminating
the need to teach the concept again later. It also increases the
likelihood that what children have learned in one lesson will help
them understand another lesson. Competence in procedures such
as calculation may be achievable through rapid drill, but thinking
takes time, and Japanese teachers strive to allow their students
time to think. Especially at the early grades, they frequently ad-
monish students not to give a hasty answer, but to slow down and
think.

In the United States, curriculum planners, textbook publishers,
and teachers themselves seem to believe that students learn more
effectively if they solve a large number of problems rather than if
they concentrate their attention on only a few. The emphasis is on
doing rather than on thinking. American teachers place a high
premium on their ability to cover a large number of problems, and
may regard that as the mark of an expert teacher. In a study
comparing expert versus novice elementary school teachers in the
United States, expert teachers were found to cover many more
mathematics problems in a single lesson than novice teachers did,
suggesting that with experience teachers grow more adept at getting students to cover a large amount of material.[2] Contrast this
with Japan and Taiwan, where teachers concentrate so intently on
only a few problems.

Covering only a few problems does not mean that a lesson turns out to be short on content. In fact, this does not appear to be the case. When many problems are covered, the same mathematical content tends to be repeated with each new problem; when fewer problems are presented, there is time for the kind of discussion that transforms the solution of problems from something that must be memorized to something that is understood.

The Japanese emphasis on reflection appears not only in mathematics. Other researchers have noted the same phenomenon in reading instruction. Jana Mason and her colleagues had this to report after studying reading instruction in forty Japanese kindergarten and primary school classrooms:

> One's first impression is that instruction is rapid-fire, with little lost motion or wasted time. We remain confident that there is a sense in which these impressions are accurate. Yet the realization eventually dawned on us that progress through stories is very slow. In one first-grade class, for instance, we saw an entire 40-minute period spent on 29 words describing a single episode from a 252-word story. We were shocked when a second-grade teacher whom we had seen teach an excellent lesson informed us in an after-school interview that his class covers about two stories a month.[3]

Teachers ask questions for different reasons in the United States and in Japan. In the United States, the purpose of a question is to get an answer. In Japan, teachers pose questions to stimulate thought. A Japanese teacher considers a question to be a poor one if it elicits an immediate answer, for this indicates that students were not challenged to think. One teacher we interviewed told us of discussions she had with her fellow teachers on how to improve teaching practices. "What do you talk about?" we wondered. "A great deal of time," she reported, "is spent talking about questions we can pose to the class—which wordings work best to get students involved in thinking and discussing the material. One good question can keep a whole class going for a long time; a bad one produces little more than a simple answer."

HANDLING DIVERSITY

Whenever we discuss our research on teaching practices, someone in the audience inevitably reminds us that Japan and China are nations with relatively homogeneous populations, whereas the United States is the melting pot of the world. How could we possibly expect that practices used in Asian societies could be relevant in the American context, where diversity in race, ethnicity, and language is so great?

The error in this question is the assumption that it is the diversity in children's social and cultural backgrounds that poses the greatest problem for teaching. In fact, a far greater problem is variability in children's educational background, and thus in their levels of preparation for learning the academic curriculum. The greater variability in mathematics achievement among American children, as compared to Japanese children, is due in large part to variability between America's neighborhoods and schools. *Within individual classrooms* the variability in levels of academic achievement differs little between the United States and Japan, Taiwan, or China. Although virtually all elementary school children learn the uniform curriculum in Asian countries, children still differ in their mastery of the subjects. Where Japan and other Asian countries have succeeded in reducing variability, they have done so by reducing the discrepancies in educational outcomes among different elementary schools. It is wrong to argue that diversity within classrooms is an American problem. Teachers everywhere must deal with students who vary in their knowledge and motivation.

How do teachers in Asian classrooms handle diversity in students' knowledge and skills? For one thing, they typically use a variety of approaches in their teaching, allowing students who may not understand one approach the opportunity to experience other ways of presenting the material. Explanations by the teacher are interspersed with periods in which children work with concrete materials or struggle to come up with their own solutions to problems. There is continuous change from one mode of presentation, one type of representation, and one teaching method to another.

Asian teaching practices thrive in the face of diversity, and some practices even depend on diversity for their effectiveness. Asking students to suggest alternative solutions to a problem, as we have observed, works best when students have had experience in generating alternative solutions. Incorrect solutions, which, as we have seen, may be dismissed by the American teacher, become topics for discussion in Asian classrooms, and all students can learn from the discussion. American schools attempt to solve the problem of diversity by segregating children into different groups or different classrooms, and by spending large amounts of regular class time working with individual students. Asian teachers believe that the only way they can cope with the problem is to devise teaching techniques that accommodate the different interests and backgrounds of the children in their classrooms.

Asian teachers also exploit the fact that the same instruction can affect different students in different ways, something that may be overlooked by American teachers. In this sense, Asian teachers subscribe to what would be considered in the West a constructivist view of learning.[4] According to this view, knowledge is regarded as something that must be constructed by the child rather than as a set of facts and skills that can be imparted by the teacher. Because children are engaged in their own construction of knowledge, some of the major tasks for the teacher are to pose provocative questions, to allow adequate time for reflection, and to vary teaching techniques so that they are responsive to differences in students' prior experience. Through such practices Asian teachers are able to accommodate individual differences in learning abilities, even though instruction is not tailored to each student.

Few who have visited urban classrooms in Asia would disagree that Chinese and Japanese teachers are highly skilled professionals. What is often not appreciated is how thoughtfully and adroitly they guide children through the vast amount of material they must master during the six years of elementary school. We of course witnessed examples of excellent teaching in American classrooms. But what has impressed us in our personal observations and in our data is how remarkably well most Asian teachers teach. It is the widespread excellence of Asian class lessons that is so stunning.

DEFINING THE PROBLEM

The techniques used by Chinese and Japanese teachers are not new to the teaching profession—nor are they foreign or exotic. In fact, they are ones often recommended by American educators. What the Chinese and Japanese examples demonstrate so compellingly is that when widely and consistently implemented, such practices can produce extraordinary outcomes.

Unfortunately, these techniques have not been broadly applied in the United States. Why? The major obstacle to the widespread development and execution of excellent lessons in America is the fact that American teachers are overworked. It would help, too, if American educators shared the belief that the whole-group lesson, if done well, can work for every child. But even if they did, it would be difficult to achieve anything near the broad-based high quality that we observed in Asian classrooms unless teachers were given time to focus on perfecting their lessons.

Lacking the training and time that are necessary to prepare lessons and the opportunities to share experiences with one another, American teachers find it difficult to organize lively, vivid, coherent lessons. Preparing well-crafted lessons takes time. Teaching them effectively requires energy. Both are in short supply for most American teachers. In the face of limitations in time for preparation and consultation and a heavy teaching load, it is surprising that American teachers teach as well as they do.

Surely the most pressing challenge in educating young children is to create new types of school environments, ones where great lessons are a commonplace occurrence. In order to do this, we must ask how we can institute reforms that will make it possible for American teachers to practice their profession under conditions more favorable for their own professional development and for the education of children.

Chapter 10

Defining the Solution

Our research in Asia has helped us to define some of the problems the United States faces as it tries to improve its educational system. Now it is time to consider possible solutions. What have we learned after spending over a decade studying other cultures? Can these lessons be helpful here?

Some of the problems we have identified were apparent without going outside our borders, and their solutions will be more or less evident once Americans acknowledge that they exist. For others, not only are the solutions elusive, but the presence of the problems themselves is not obvious. During our decade of research, we have been astonished to realize how many of the problems we would have missed if we had studied only American schools and families. Only when we examined the beliefs, attitudes, and behavior of Americans in the context of other cultures did we find that some of what we, like most Americans, had regarded as natural and normal suddenly appeared odd or inexplicable.

We recognize the importance of caution when we speak of possible solutions to America's distressing problems in education.

What works in one culture will not necessarily work in another, and Americans are not interested in mimicking Asia. It is easy, for example, to suggest that we should extend the school day from the American 180 days to the Asian 240 days, but we doubt that this change alone would either improve children's achievement or increase their enjoyment of school. On the other hand, having seen the way a longer school year is used by Asians, we may be in a better position to evaluate its application to the American scene. Just as Asians adapted many practices from the West so that they served the Asian cultures well, Americans can look at Asian practices to see if some of them can be adapted to serve our purposes.

INTRODUCING REFORM

Before the United States can begin meaningful educational reform, we Americans must decide what we expect of our students. Do we place a high value on academic achievement? Or do we give other goals, such as being popular or a good athlete, a higher priority? Because American educational policy is not made at a national level, there has been little nationwide discussion or debate about these issues. As a result, there is no national consensus. States, school systems, and individual schools are trying to introduce educational reforms, but their efforts are scattered and uncoordinated. Even within states, we see acrimonious controversy about "no pass, no play" rules for athletes, literacy tests for high school diplomas, and other reform measures.

The closest American approach in recent years to a national discussion was the meeting in 1989 of the governors and President Bush to establish "ambitious national educational goals—performance goals that must be achieved if the United States is to remain competitive in the world marketplace and our citizens are to reach their fullest potential."[1] The country is no closer to realizing those ambitious goals today than it was when they were announced. War, recession, and other matters have drawn national attention away from education. This is unfortunate, for the country will continue to suffer the consequences of mediocre schools until Americans are clearer about what we really want from our public schools. At present, wide-scale confusion exists about nearly all aspects of education, including its function in a democracy, its financial support, and the control of educational policy.

The time has come when the United States needs a national education policy. We need a national consensus about how educational policy should be made and how control should be divided among federal, state, and local agencies. We need to discuss the form that this policy should take. We must decide who should control the curriculum. Are Americans willing to abdicate this function to textbook publishers, who follow the demands of a few powerful state adoption committees? Should curricula conform to a national standard, delineated through guidelines and sets of accomplishments that all children are expected to meet? Or does state or local control of the curriculum remain the most effective way to prepare students for the working world?

These questions are complex, and they generate heated disagreement. But without a clearer mission, our public schools are likely to continue to be sources of disillusionment and targets of criticism as they struggle to achieve the ever-changing, poorly articulated, and conflicting goals imposed upon them by the American public.

Despite their shortcomings, national standards would go a long way toward bringing order to our present chaotic curricula. Children would no longer be rewarded or penalized for moving, teachers would have clear frameworks for organizing their lessons, publishers could plan better texts with assurance of their acceptability, and parents would be able to evaluate their children's progress with less guesswork. Adopting national guidelines and standards does not necessarily mean relinquishing local control. School districts could still decide the manner in which they would follow the guidelines and attempt to meet these standards.

The Function of Schools

Americans have many goals for their children. We all want our children to be intellectually competent, socially adept, and emotionally secure. And we increasingly expect schools to take the responsibility for these outcomes. As a result, tasks traditionally assumed by families have been dumped into the lap of the schools, and the schools' mission has become more diffusely defined. Public school personnel can hardly continue to function as counselors, psychologists, special educators, and parent surrogates as well as expert teachers. Schools may not be the most appropriate providers of services that homes and communities once delivered. Other agencies must take on more of the responsibility. At the very least, we should be honest about our expectations and either provide schools with the financial support necessary to meet these obligations, or cease depending upon schools to solve so many of our children's problems.

Some citizens criticize schools as dreary places that teach subject matter only and neglect teaching students how to think. Others despair at the newfangled curricula and long to return to a core curriculum from which topics such as life problems and social issues are excluded. According to some critics, moral education should be given a more central place in academic curricula, but other citizens are staunchly opposed on the grounds that this is the function of the home and of community institutions, not of schools.

Other nations have attempted to define their educational goals. Every child in China knows that (in order of importance) "the purpose of education in the People's Republic of China is moral, intellectual, and physical development." Sometimes the order is switched, so that intellectual development takes precedence over moral development, but the goals themselves have been constant for many years. The goals in Taiwan are more specific. Article 158 of the Constitution of the Republic of China states: "Education shall aim at the development of the national spirit, the spirit of self-government, national morality, a healthy physique, scientific knowledge and the ability to earn a living."[2] The Japanese are even more specific. They provide goals for each aspect of education. The Ministry of Education's course guide defines overall objectives for elementary schools, and then elaborates the goals for each subject—from reading and science to homemaking and physical education. These goals are defined separately for each grade and are accompanied by detailed descriptions of how these goals can be accomplished. American schools cannot hope to develop programs and curricula that will meet these goals when they remain diffuse and ill-defined.

Schools in a Democracy

There is confusion about whether schools serve democracy best by trying to provide all children with the same educational opportunities or by tailoring education to meet the needs of special groups. Schools designed for the average child may not meet the special needs of the severely mentally retarded, emotionally disturbed, or learning disabled. It is necessary to have special classes or schools for these children. However, within the normal range, some students simply learn more slowly than their peers. At first glance it may appear humane to expect less of these children and to put them in classes or groups for slow learners. But then they are offered a less demanding curriculum than that of their classmates, and as a consequence are deprived of any possibility of catching up and of being able to compete in their future search for jobs.

Highly able students constitute another special group. To what degree can or should schools foster the training of an intellectual elite—groups of future scientists, engineers, and other professionals who will lead the United States in scientific and technological advances in the next century? Can we provide special opportunities for these students without reducing opportunities for much larger numbers of their less gifted peers?

When we talk about our comparative research, we are often

challenged by someone who asks how, if the system is so bad, it can produce so many Nobel prizewinners. We point out that Americans allocate resources to create a thin layer of the population that is extraordinarily well educated and highly skilled. But this is only a veneer. The great majority of the population—the ordinary citizens—typically do not have access to an education that prepares them well for full participation in the country's economy and political system. Our nation is being polarized by inequities in the quality of educational opportunities. Until all students are provided with equal access to an effective education, this polarization will continue. We cannot afford to ignore our highly able students or other students with special needs, but meeting their needs must not occur at the cost of depriving the vast majority of children of the education they need and deserve.

A Problem of Money?

A ready explanation for many of America's social problems, including those in education, is that they result from a lack of money. Yet the United States has one of the largest financial investments in education of any country in the world. In 1987, for example, average per-pupil expenditure for education from kindergarten through twelfth grade ($3,398) was behind that of only five other industrialized nations: Sweden, Canada, Denmark, Switzerland, and Norway.[3] Yet we are producing students who cannot compete with those of nations such as China, a developing country, or Japan, which spends less than 3 percent of its gross national product on elementary and secondary education, compared to more than 4 percent in the United States.[4] More money alone will not solve the problems. If we spend more just to continue what we are doing now, both citizens and legislators will inevitably be deeply disappointed in the return on their investment.

On the other hand, an assessment of how current resources could be reallocated is in order. In 1959, teachers' salaries accounted for 56 percent of the operating budgets of American public schools. By 1989, the percentage had dropped to 40.4 percent.[5] Most of the decline is due to increased salaries for special personnel and administrators. These statistics are shocking. We do not wish to argue that the service personnel in the public schools fail to serve a useful purpose. What these statistics reveal is that more than half of the funds allocated to education are not being spent on the schools' fundamental function: teaching children.

WHAT CAN WE DO?

Some of the difficulties lie in the American schools themselves, but schools alone are not the source of all the problems. The disengagement of American families from their children's education causes many other serious difficulties. Perhaps the most intractable obstacle to improving public education is American society itself. Some of the beliefs, attitudes, and practices common among Americans dampen and at times even destroy the enthusiasm and motivation of both teachers and students. The most difficult, but essential, question we must raise is how can we change our educational goals and practices given the nature of American society.

In the following pages we try to suggest what we Americans can do to improve education and to make learning a more exciting quest for all children. We do not accept easy explanations, such as the suggestion that American children's poor achievement is due to their having lower IQs than their Asian peers, to their attending schools with inadequate physical facilities, or to their watching too much television. Superficial explanations deflect us from thinking about more fundamental issues, most of which have to do with teachers, parents, and society in general. Some of our suggestions are modest; others are much bolder.

CHANGING THE SCHOOLS

A teacher recently confronted us with the following question: "Okay, let's say that you could do one thing to improve education. What would it be?" We had a hard time choosing only one of several changes in American schooling that we believe are critically needed. Therefore we made several suggestions.

Free Teachers

The first thing we would recommend is to decrease the teaching load of American elementary school teachers. Until teachers have *adequate time* to prepare lessons, work outside of class with individual students, and perfect their teaching practices by interacting with each other and with master teachers, it is going to be difficult, if not impossible, to change what children learn and do in school.

We doubt that we would have made this recommendation before we began our comparative studies. It was not apparent to us, and we believe it is not apparent to most Americans, that elementary school teachers in American schools are required to spend too much time in the classroom. When we witnessed the dynamic teaching in Chinese and Japanese classrooms and began to find out what was behind it, we were hit full force with the reason why much elementary school teaching in the United States is unimpressive. It is inconceivable that American teachers, by themselves, would be able to organize lively, vivid, coherent lessons under a regimen that requires them to teach hour after hour every day throughout the school year.

As long as teachers are in front of a classroom for hours on end, we cannot expect to find the versatility, energy, and inventiveness needed to rejuvenate American education. It is a tribute to American teachers' dedication and love of children that so many remain in the profession and find it a continuing source of gratification.

Freeing teachers from some of the hours they spend in the classroom would allow them time for professional development and would help to reduce the isolation that pervades the lives of too many of them. With more time to prepare lessons, to correct children's work, and to plan activities, both by themselves and with their colleagues, teachers' classroom performance—and in turn, the performance of the children—could be more consistent, thorough, and dynamic. Providing large rooms where teachers can meet and work together would foster more frequent interaction among teachers and reduce their isolation.

Improve Teacher Training

More than free time is needed to revolutionize American teaching practices. Teachers need to be better trained. Rather than spending large amounts of time on the philosophy and theories of teaching, teachers need help in learning the practical techniques of effective instruction. Good teachers develop over a long time, and their development must be given greater attention. In order to help teachers improve the quality of their teaching, much of their training must be shifted from university lecture halls to school classrooms.

Other professions place aspiring professionals in practical settings as soon as they have been exposed to the basic information around which the profession is built. Medical educators, for example, demand that future physicians spend large amounts of time in the clinic and hospital room during their years in medical school, at first observing, and then, under the supervision of an experienced physician, gradually taking on more and more responsibility for the treatment of patients. A similar model can be productively applied to training teachers. Currently, practice teaching occurs under the supervision of already overburdened classroom teachers, and observation of practice teachers seldom extends to more than a few hours a semester. Opportunities for observing and emulating the practices of outstanding models and for practicing under the supervision of skilled teachers would provide the kinds of experience that all good professionals need.

Skilled teachers need to be relieved of some of their routine duties so they can help their young colleagues. Working with these experienced teachers would be a welcome alternative to many of the courses in methods that students in colleges of education are required to take, courses that we have often heard described as full of dull banter and belaboring the obvious. Future teachers could then spend more of their time at the university taking courses in the basic disciplines of mathematics, literature, history, social sciences, and other fundamental subjects. To be able to organize clear, authoritative, coherent lessons and to improvise when children think of unusual questions or unexpected solutions requires solid mastery of basic subject matter. It seems self-evident that the more teachers know about what they are teaching, the more they can contribute to their students.

Make Systematic Use of Learning Principles

A common excuse for inadequate achievement is that there is insufficient information as a basis for action. This is not the case in education. We already know a great deal about the principles of human learning. The kinds of principles that seem to be so effectively implemented in Asian classrooms are ones most American educators would agree with. What we do not know is how to put them into wider practice. Here are some widely accepted examples of rules about learning that should lead to good teaching.

There is evidence that children learn most effectively when they:

- have a teacher who leads them to make discoveries that underlie further acquisition of knowledge and to make generalizations to other material;
- are presented with lessons that are well scripted and well

209

organized, and that use multiple approaches to illustrating the principles or ideas being taught;
- are given an idea of why they are learning certain material, and the material is presented in a context with which they have had some experience;
- are given frequent opportunities during the course of learning to interact with other children in generating ideas, explaining answers, and evaluating the adequacy of their own and other children's answers;
- are provided with clear information about the relevance and accuracy of their answers, and are not made wary of trying new ideas because mistakes are interpreted as failure;
- have hands-on experience with the material being discussed, and have the opportunity to see how the principles are derived before they are discussed in abstract terms or are formalized;
- are presented with multiple examples of a concept so that they can deduce the underlying principle, and are required to come up with some of the steps toward the solution themselves;
- are provided with opportunities to practice what they have been taught.

The list could go on and on. These ideas about learning—and the many others we have not listed—are not new. In fact, most American teachers would say they practice these principles every day. The clear difference between them and their Asian colleagues is in how consistently and how thoroughly they follow principles of good teaching—not that Chinese and Japanese teachers have discovered something the rest of the world has never known.

Teach to the Group

Teachers are responsible for developing instructional techniques that will benefit the greatest number of children in their classes. At the same time, they are expected to meet the needs of children who require special attention and help. These dual demands are an impossible burden for most American teachers. Teachers know that the class time they spend with individual children deprives the rest of the children of opportunities for instruction, but they also know that they have little time outside of class to work with children who are having problems.

There are two solutions to this dilemma. We have already suggested one: freeing teachers of some of their classroom duties. The second solution is more difficult to accomplish, because it would require modifying current teaching practices. Rather than teaching different lessons to different groups of children and thereby limiting the time any one group spends with the teacher, teachers should try to spend as much time as possible working with the whole class. Children would spend less time alone in seatwork, and teachers could employ a wider variety of activities, media, and materials.

Large individual differences among children mean that different children will benefit to different degrees from the various techniques. All students can benefit to some degree, but certain children find it easier to follow written examples, and others learn more rapidly through listening; some are better able to learn by working alone, whereas others are more successful when they work in groups. The likelihood that all children will profit from each day's lesson can be maximized if teachers vary their approaches to teaching, particularly in presenting new material. Class discussion, manipulation of concrete materials, group solution of problems, and other techniques that all teachers use at times would increase children's understanding and add to the liveliness of the class if they were introduced more frequently.

When classes are broken up into small groups for cooperative activities, children would be more likely to learn from each other if all levels of ability were represented in each group. Slower learners would benefit from posing questions to the faster learners, and faster learners would benefit from having to think about how to answer them.

Consider Increasing Class Size

A notion popular among both parents and teachers is that higher achievement would result if the number of students assigned to each classroom were decreased. We wonder, however, whether it is the size of the class per se or the amount of work that is involved in teaching that contributes to this recommendation. Would teachers object to teaching somewhat larger classes if they had the time and energy to handle them, and if they were trained to use techniques of whole-group instruction that are known to work? Would they agree to increasing class size a bit if it meant that they would have more time each day to plan lessons, deal with individual children, and consult with colleagues?

No clear relationship has been established between size of class and pupil achievement, as former Secretary of Education William Bennett pointed out in his report on elementary education in the United States.[6] We believe that many improvements in elementary school education could be accomplished if the average class size were slightly increased and the savings used to expand teachers' opportunities for perfecting their teaching and for interacting with other teachers.

There is a number below which it is probably not cost-effective to reduce the size of American classes, and one above which teachers would be overburdened. These numbers probably range between 25 and 35 pupils, and depend on the school. Class size needs to be reduced in schools that enroll large numbers of students with severe problems, but in many more it could be increased—to the benefit of teachers.

Revise Textbooks

We have pointed out that American textbooks tend to be excessively long, repetitive, and distracting and underestimate what children can understand. Rather than believing that children can be active participants in the construction of their own knowledge, many textbook writers offer curricula that depend more on memorization than on understanding, and on offering step-by-step solutions to problems than on enabling students to create their own solutions to novel problems. Curricula need not return year after year to the same material, and textbooks could challenge children at all levels of knowledge and ability.

Workbooks and teachers' manuals, in addition to textbooks, form the core of much classroom instruction. American workbooks for children tend to be dull repetitions of every detail of the lessons, and teachers' manuals are often as simplistic in their step-by-step approach to teaching. Far too little attention has been paid to the development of these tools. As is the case with teaching, we know enough to produce good workbooks and teaching manuals; where we are remiss is in putting what we know into practice.

Free Children

Children, like their teachers, need to spend more of the school day outside of the classroom. The American practice of requiring children to remain in the classroom most of the day almost guarantees a reduction in the joy of learning. Complaints about hyperactivity and irrelevant activity among American children offer clear cues that we are asking children to sit still for too many hours every day. Brief breaks during which children stand and stretch or do exercises in the hall are insufficient. Recovery from the task of listening and learning hour after hour requires regularly spaced intervals of vigorous play. One wonders how often the currently popular biological explanations of behavior disorders result in

213

diagnoses of minimal brain damage in children who simply need to have more opportunities for physical exercise and release of tension.

Recesses not only allow for physical recovery, they also help to make school a place where children can interact socially with their friends. Typical programming in American elementary schools does not meet children's needs for social interaction and group membership. Schools often appear to be lonely, even harsh places, and children become increasingly disengaged from school the longer they are in attendance. Additional recesses, longer lunch periods, and more after-school programs would automatically increase opportunities for play and social interaction, and schools would become more comfortable settings for children.

Would young children establish closer friendships and enjoy school more if they were kept together in the same group with the same teacher for longer? This is not a foreign concept; earlier in the century it was a common practice in small schoolhouses throughout the country for children and teachers to remain together for two, three, or even more years. This practice needs to be re-examined as a way of promoting school as an enjoyable, socially supportive institution, a rewarding place for children to go about the business of learning.

Eliminate Tracking

Children with major handicaps cannot benefit from many of the activities of the regular classroom; they clearly require special forms of instruction. However, separating other elementary school children into different tracks or groups according to ability seems unproductive. For slow learners, the stigma of being classified as slow learners or children with problems, along with the reduced opportunities to learn from interactions with their peers in regular classrooms, may greatly reduce the advantages that are supposed to follow from being placed in a special group or special class. Nor are there special advantages for faster learners; there is little evi-

214

dence that they learn less in classrooms containing children of all levels of ability.

The argument that children need to be separated by levels of ability or enrolled in special education classes would be more convincing if it could be demonstrated that they could not learn in the regular classroom, even under optimal conditions. This would be hard to show. Although teachers may be sensitive to the educational needs of individual children, the conditions under which they currently teach make it impossible for them to satisfy these needs, and so the "exceptional" children are separated from their peers. Rather than giving these young children a proper start in their schooling, this practice launches them on an ever diverging pathway from which they will be unlikely to find their way back to a regular classroom.

Respect the Age of Innocence

In their zeal to prepare their children properly for school, many Americans want to introduce academic work earlier and earlier into their children's lives. Nursery schools are being asked to begin pre-reading and pre-arithmetic classes; there is a push to begin classes for four-year-olds in the public schools; and having a head start in school is now translated as knowing the alphabet and the fundamentals of reading and mathematics. But are the preschool years an appropriate time for formal instruction, or can more be accomplished by informal introduction into the world of numbers and words?

There may be some advantages in this early teaching, but there are dangers as well. Children, not yet having developed a wish to learn academic material themselves, may tire of being asked to perform in order to please their teachers and parents. The preschool years, we believe, should be a time when children learn to interact with their peers and with adults other than their parents, to experience the exhilaration of freely exploring the world around them, and to master the routines that will make their life in elementary school less stressful. Experiences in Asia, where there is little formal academic teaching in preschool and kindergarten, show us that it is not necessary to concentrate on early academic preparation in order to develop high-achieving children.

WHAT FAMILIES CAN DO

The behavior and attitudes of parents are critical to children's performance in school. Although American schools will and should bear the heaviest burden of change if children's achievement is to show radical improvement, efforts at school reform cannot be fully effective unless American parents become more involved in their children's education and develop appropriate expectations about what their children can accomplish.

From the first grade on, American children tend to live in two worlds that have little to do with each other. Teachers often feel alienated from parents, and many parents feel unwanted by teachers. The estrangement between school and home has not served children well. When parents feel that they have nothing to contribute to their children's education because they don't understand "new math," "new science," or "reading for meaning" programs, they naturally begin to turn more and more responsibility over to the schools. At the same time, teachers, struggling to master the newest fashions in curricula, find few opportunities to help parents become more involved in their children's schoolwork.

The separation of parents from their children's schools has also come about because of parents' confused perceptions about the role they should play in their children's education. Parents' conviction that they are not home-based teacher surrogates is well advised, but this does not mean that they should avoid any involvement. Whether or not they are able to help with homework, they can express curiosity about the subjects their children are

216

studying. They can demonstrate an interest in their children's academic life at school. "Show-and-tell" times at school encourage children to bring some of their everyday experiences into the classroom. The equivalent of show-and-tell times at home would allow children to share their school experiences and give them a sense that their life at school is important to the family.

Parents can create a physical and psychological environment at home that is conducive to study. Providing space or a desk at which to work indicates the seriousness with which parents regard their children's education. Parents can indicate that they consider schoolwork to be an integral part of children's daily routines by organizing the day so that time is set aside for studying. Linkages between school and home can also be strengthened if parents regularly visit their children's schools and become acquainted with their children's teachers—something that now happens less and less frequently, the longer American children are in school. It is unclear whether this is because parents become increasingly alienated from the schools or because they lose interest in the role they can play or are allowed to play in their children's education.

Many American parents appear to believe that they can meet their educational obligations mainly by being enthusiastic about their children's accomplishments and emotionally supportive when children confront difficulties. But children need stronger indications of parental interest and concern. Rather than becoming disengaged from education once their children enter school, American parents should preserve the high level of involvement that they show during the preschool years. Unless they demonstrate that they value education and are willing to become involved in what goes on at school, their children will continue to regard school as a place that is generally unconnected to the main events of their lives.

Make Realistic Assessments and Raise Standards

Americans are an expansive people. What is "good" in another country tends to be "great" in the United States. The buoyant optimism that is promoted by such attitudes has carried our country far, but there are signs that more realistic appraisals would better prepare the nation for the next century. Data from several thousand interviews with American mothers in our studies indicate that they really believe that their abilities and those of their children generally are "above average," and that their children are doing well in school and possess "much above average" prospects for the future. The great majority of mothers were uncritical of their children's performance, were satisfied with the education their children were receiving, and had few suggestions for improving teaching.

Americans are satisfied with their children's education partly because they have lacked a meaningful gauge by which to evaluate how well their children are doing. Because most children pass from one grade to the next, and parents see smiley faces rather than grades on many of their children's assignments, they assume that their children are doing a good job. This clearly is not true. The results of cross-national studies now provide standards for achievement against which American children's performance can be compared. Although American parents seem unaware of their children's deficiencies, the results of the studies are so consistent and cover such a broad range of ages that we have no alternative but to recognize or admit that American students are not competitive with those of many other nations.

Another American characteristic that has led to high satisfaction with education is a tendency to underestimate what children are capable of accomplishing in school. Convincing parents that they can expect more of their children is difficult, however, for it quickly becomes confused with pushing children too early and too fast. We are not proposing that children should be taught to read in preschool, or that they should be doing algebra in fifth grade.

What we *are* saying is that lessons do not need to be repeated year after year if they are properly taught in the first place; that children can master school routines if someone takes the time to show them how; that children can comprehend far more complicated material than they learn now if it commands their interest and is explained clearly; and that most children are capable, given the proper instruction, of mastering the academic curriculum.

Parents' reluctance to raise their expectations may be based on a fear that higher parental expectations lead to higher levels of stress in children. There is no evidence to support this fear. We have not found great stress among Asian elementary school children, and there is no reason to believe that it would increase here. Meeting reasonable challenges enhances self-confidence and self-esteem; lack of challenge accomplishes little. Americans accept this precept in athletic achievement—surely the same principles apply to academic achievement.

We are left with the depressing conclusion that American parents' low academic standards and their tendency to overestimate their children's accomplishments work strongly against children's motivation for high academic achievement. If a parent erroneously believes that a child is doing well and communicates this impression to him or her, the child may see no purpose in studying harder. It is paradoxical that positive attitudes could in fact undermine children's motivation to strive hard in their studies, but when mothers' satisfaction with their children's abilities and achievement is inflated, the message conveyed is that things are going well enough and there is no apparent need to do better.

CHANGING SOCIAL BELIEFS

A belief in the value of education for all people is a fundamental tenet of American democracy. During recent decades, however, the commitment to this belief appears to have weakened. Americans do not seem to believe that all children are capable of benefiting from regular schooling. They appear to believe that even with hard work, some children are doomed to low levels of achievement. Such beliefs constitute one of the greatest impediments to reaching the national goals for education proposed by the governors and the President.

It would be impractical to hope that these beliefs would change, except for the fact that they are alien to the American heritage. It is often pointed out that this country was built on the belief that all citizens should have equal opportunities for advancement and that they should be able to achieve their goals through hard work—a belief that was the basis for establishing universal education in the United States in the last century.

Value Education

It is not at all clear that most Americans really believe that providing good schools is one of the most productive investments a nation can make. Nor is it clear, judging from the lack of interest in school and the large number of high school dropouts, that most American students regard schoolwork as the most productive use of their time.

Among the groups for whom education and educational reform have become a strong concern, however, is American business. Faced with the need to bring large numbers of workers up to a level of competence that will enable them to work effectively, American business groups have become some of the strongest advocates for improvements in education. For example, they have formed the Business Roundtable Education Task Force, whose members represent two hundred of the nation's leading corporations. John Akers, chairman of IBM and of the Task Force, expressed the high value he and his colleagues place on education in a recent article written for *The Wall Street Journal:*

American business has the resources, the people and the commitment to help this country's schools regain, and indeed surpass, their performance and prestige of old. Our democratic system depends on a well-educated citizenry. So let's agree on what must be done, and work with America's students, their parents, teachers and principals.[7]

Despite the recent national attention given to educational reform by business, some political groups, and a few other groups with a vested interest in improving education, the public generally remains indifferent. Perhaps what has not been apparent to many citizens is that everyone's future is affected by the quality of American education. Funds and attention should not be perceived as simply aiding the advancement of someone else's children. Rather, we are investing in future fellow citizens, whose skill and knowledge will determine whether the country will maintain its economic prosperity or whether it will fall behind nations that have been more astute in analyzing and meeting their human needs. Unless Americans can make the changes that will lead us to be proud of our schools, to hold our teachers in high esteem, and to decide that there is no better way for our children and teenagers to spend part of every day than in studying, we will have squandered the nation's potential for future excellence.

Believe in Effort

Perhaps the most self-defeating belief that has taken hold in the United States during recent decades concerns the relative contributions of innate ability and effort to achievement. Early in our country's history, probably as part of the Protestant work ethic, people believed they could achieve almost anything with enough effort. We have gradually come to emphasize the limits on what can be accomplished imposed by innate differences among individuals. There are—and always will be—individual differences among human beings in whatever characteristics are measured. But this variability should not be interpreted to mean that the general level of accomplishment cannot be raised. Why dwell on the fact that some students will do better than others, when the whole distribution of scores is depressed? The worst Chinese students in mathematics received scores that were near the average for American students!

A person's willingness to expend effort depends on whether he or she believes the effort is worthwhile. Those who suggest that not all children are capable of mastering the elementary school curriculum because of differences in innate ability are engaged in a self-fulfilling prophecy by depriving them of the opportunity to learn with and from their fellow students. Espousing a position that effectively limits the accomplishments of certain members of the population is a serious obstacle to introducing change. The "miracle" of Asian economic development is no less impressive than the "miracle" of Asian children's academic achievement. Behind both of these so-called miracles is the conviction that accomplishment depends on dedication and hard work. By assuming that all children are able to learn effectively if they are taught well and work hard, Asians have enhanced the achievement of all their children.

Examples from the United States can also be cited that call into question the restrictive power of presumed limits imposed by innate ability. Record after record has been shattered in sports not because of genetic changes in human potential, but because of improvements in the physical condition of the athletes, their training, and the skill of their coaches. Stereotypes have also been destroyed in other areas. It would have been inconceivable thirty years ago that a youth with Down's syndrome could star in a popular television series. The status of people with Down's syndrome has steadily improved during recent years, partly because of the discovery that, with effort, they could learn more effectively than had been supposed. Similarly, teachers in East Los Angeles high schools would have dismissed the suggestion that their Chicano students could become high achievers in mathematics until Jaime Escalante demonstrated that with dedication, self-confidence, and hard work, potential high school dropouts could excel on advanced placement tests of college entrance examinations. Of course there are limits to what different people are capable of achieving, but we should make no uninformed assumptions about what these limits are.

The belief in the importance of hard work is not alien to Americans. The mystery is why, in the later years of the twentieth century, we have modified this belief in such a destructive way. Why do we dwell on the differences among us, rather than on our similarities? Why are we unwilling to see that the whole society is advanced when all of its members, not only privileged socioeconomic and ethnic groups, are given the opportunity to use their abilities to their fullest? How much more strongly do we need to be shocked by data that herald decline in our children's academic achievement before we devote ourselves wholeheartedly and sincerely to the improvement of the education we give our children at home and at school?

The American educational system as it currently exists is producing an educationally advantaged minority and a disadvantaged majority. The outcome is the perpetuation and amplification of socioeconomic differences and potential conflict within the population. Asian educational systems, on the other hand, give the great majority of citizens about the same educational start in life and tend toward social equality. Such social and political benefits may in the long run prove to be important for both the health of a nation and its economic competitiveness.

POSTSCRIPT

We are often asked if we think the situation is hopeless—that the lack of consensus, multiple goals, and diffusion of power makes it impossible for American public schools *ever* to function effectively. We do not think it is hopeless, but two sets of data we have recently collected indicate that the attention given to education during the past decade has not yet alerted Americans to the size of the task.

At the University of Michigan we are now completing two new

large studies. One compares the performance of fifth-graders over the past decade, and the other is a follow-up study of the children we initially met in 1980 when they were first-graders. For the first study, we returned to the same elementary schools in Minneapolis, Sendai, and Taipei that we had visited in our earlier studies. Once again we assessed fifth-graders' achievement and their mothers' evaluations of their children's education. The American fifth-graders were just as far below their Chinese and Japanese peers in academic achievement as they had been during the earlier testing periods. Moreover, American children held just as high an opinion of their own abilities as they had a decade earlier, and their mothers were no more aware of the problems concerning education than the American mothers had been in 1980. The American mothers continued to be satisfied with their children's performance and with the job their children's school was doing.

Three years after they leave elementary school nearly all the students in Minneapolis and Sendai enter high school; in Taipei, some of the students enter vocational schools or leave school for a job. The first-graders we studied in 1980 are now in the eleventh grade. We know already that eleven years after they entered elementary school, the American students are even further behind their Chinese and Japanese peers in academic achievement than they were in first or fifth grade.

Endnotes

1. Introduction

1. Kearns, D. (1989). Improving the workforce: Competitiveness begins at school. *The New York Times*, December 17, 1989, 2.
2. Spiro, M. E. (1990). On the strange and the familiar in recent anthropological thought. In J. W. Stigler, R. A. Shweder, and G. Herdt, eds., *Cultural psychology: Essays on comparative human development*. New York: Cambridge University Press, pp. 47–61.
3. *Chicago Tribune*, February 16, 1987.
4. Grosvenor, G. M. (1987). Geographic education: An investment in your students' future. Paper presented at the Annual Meeting of the American Association of School Administrators, New Orleans.
5. Fallows, J. (1989). *More like us: Making America great again*. New York: Houghton Mifflin.
6. Our most recent evidence comes from a current Michigan study of eleventh-graders in Japan, Taiwan, and the United States. There was no greater indication of self-reported stress, depression, or psychosomatic disorders among the Chinese and Japanese than among the American students.
7. U. S. Department of Education (1990). *National goals for education*. Washington, D. C.: U. S. Department of Education.
8. Cremin, L. A. (1990). *Popular education and its discontents*. New York: Harper and Row.

2. Academic Achievement

1. Hoffman, R. (1989). Ignorance, ignorantly judged. *The New York Times,* September 14, 1989, A29.

2. Greenfield, J. (1991). Officially Important Survey is moronic, not America's schoolchildren. *Ann Arbor News,* June 9, 1991, D13.

3. Husen, T. (1967). *International study of achievement in mathematics.* New York: Wiley.

4. McKnight, C. C., Crosswhite, F. J., Dossey, J. A., Kifer, E., Swafford, J. O., Travers, K. J., and Cooney, T. J. (1987). *The underachieving curriculum: Assessing U.S. school mathematics from an international perspective.* Champaign, IL: Stipes.

5. National Research Council (1989). *Everybody counts: A report to the nation on the future of mathematics education.* Washington, D. C.: National Academy Press.

6. LaPointe, A. E., Mead, N. A., and Phillips, G. W. (1989). *A world of differences: An international assessment of mathematics and science.* Princeton, N. J.: Educational Testing Service.

7. Cremin, L. A. (1990). *Popular education and its discontents.* New York: Harper and Row.

8. Stevenson, H. W., Lee, S. Y., and Stigler, J. W. (1986). Mathematics achievement of Chinese, Japanese, and American children. *Science, 231,* 693–699; Stigler, J. W., Lee, S. Y., Lucker, G. W., and Stevenson, H. W. (1982). Curriculum and achievement in mathematics: A study of elementary school children in Japan, Taiwan, and the United States. *Journal of Educational Psychology, 74,* 315–322.

9. Stevenson, H. W., Lee, S. Y., Chen, C., Lummis, M., Stigler, J., Fan, L., and Ge, F. (1990). Mathematics achievement of children in China and the United States. *Child Development, 61,* 1053–1066; Stevenson, H. W., Lee, S., Chen, C., Stigler, J. W., Hsu, C. C., and Kitamura, S. (1990). Contexts of achievement: A study of American, Chinese, and Japanese children. *Monographs of the Society for Research in Child Development, 221:55,* 1–2; Stigler, J. W., Lee, S. Y., and Stevenson, H. W. (1990). *Mathematical knowledge of Japanese, Chinese, and American*

elementary school children. Reston, VA: National Council of Teachers of Mathematics.

10. The central governments of both Taiwan and mainland China establish the mathematics curriculum for their schools and publish the single textbook series that must be used in all elementary schools. The Japanese Ministry of Education also defines a single curriculum for the country's schools, but has relinquished the publication of textbooks to private companies, whose textbooks are necessarily quite similar to each other. We chose the two most popular Japanese series for our analyses. In the United States, the content of textbooks is determined in a much less centralized fashion, and is the product of the forces of a free market and a combination of state and local guidelines. We chose the series that were most commonly used in Minneapolis and in Chicago at the times the tests were constructed.

11. Six boys and six girls from each classroom in both the first and second studies.

12. Lynn's arguments are summarized in: Lynn, R. (1982). IQ in Japan and the United States shows a growing disparity. *Nature, 297,* 222–223.

13. Stevenson, H. W. and Azuma, H. (1983). IQ in Japan and the United States: Methodological problems in Lynn's analysis. *Nature, 306,* 291–292.

14. Stevenson, H. W., Stigler, J. W., Lee, S. Y., Lucker, G. W., Kitamura, S., and Hsu, C. C. (1985). Cognitive performance and achievement of Japanese, Chinese, and American children. *Child Development, 56,* 718–734.

3. Children's Lives

1. Time estimates in this chapter are generally stated in terms of hours per week. The standard error of these estimates, averaged across categories of activity, is plus or minus twenty-two minutes per week.

Endnotes

4. Socialization and Achievement

1. Peak, L. (1991). *Learning to go to school: The transition from home to preschool life*. Berkeley: University of California Press, p. 7
2. Ridley, C. P., Godwin, P. H. B., and Doolin, D. J. (1971). *The making of a model citizen in Communist China*. Stanford, CA: Stanford University Press.
3. Lewis, C. C. (1989). From indulgence to internalization: Social control in the early years. *Journal of Japanese Studies, 15,* 139–157.

5. Effort and Ability

1. Azuma, H., Kashiwagi, K., and Hess, R. D. (1981). *Hahaoya no taido koudo to kodomo no chiteki hattatsu* (The effect of mother's attitude and behavior on the cognitive development of the child: A U.S.-Japanese comparison). Tokyo: University of Tokyo Press.
2. Terman, L. M. (1925). *Genetic studies of genius. Vol. 1. Mental and physical traits of a thousand gifted children*. Stanford, CA: Stanford University Press.
3. Gates, A. I. (1921). Educational psychology at the Chicago meetings of scientific societies. *The Journal of Educational Psychology, 12* (2), 63–71.
4. Quoted in: Watson, B. (1967). *Basic writings of Mo Tzu, Hsun Tzu, and Han Fei Tzu*. New York: Columbia University Press, p. 18.
5. Ridley, C. P., Godwin, P. H. B., and Doolin, D. J. (1971). *The making of a model citizen in Communist China*. Stanford, CA: Stanford University Press, p. 263.
6. Allington, R. L. (1984). Content coverage and contextual reading in reading groups. *Journal of Reading Behavior, 16,* 85–96.
7. Schoenfeld, A. H. (1985). *Mathematical problem solving*. Orlando, FL: Academic Press.
8. Hofstadter, R. (1963). *Anti-intellectualism in American life*. New York: Alfred A. Knopf.
9. Ibid., p.331.
10. Ibid., p.335.

11. Ibid., p.336.
12. Ibid., p.341.
13. Ibid., p.344.
14. Tsuchimochi, G. H. (1989). Education reform under the American Occupation: Report of the United States Education Mission to Japan and the Reform of the School System. *Toyo Eiwa Journal of the Humanities and Social Sciences, 1,* 65–80.
15. Coles, G. (1987). *The learning mystique: A critical look at learning disabilities.* New York: Pantheon Books.

6. Satisfactions and Expectations

1. Cannell, J. J. (1988). Nationally normed elementary achievement testing in America's public schools: How all 50 states are above the national average. *Educational Measurement: Issues and Practice, 7,* 5–15.
2. National Commission on Children (1991). *Beyond rhetoric: A new American agenda for children and families.* Washington, D. C.: U. S. Government Printing Office.
3. *Sorifu seishonen taisaku hombu. Seishonen hakubo.* [White paper on children and youth.] (1983). Tokyo: Okurasho Insatsukyoku.
4. Tatsuno, S. M. (1990). *Created in Japan.* New York: Harper & Row.

7. The Organization of Schooling

1. For a discussion of financial support of education in China see: World Bank (1985). *China: Issues and prospects in education, Annex 1.* Washington, D. C.: The World Bank.
2. Gardner, H. (October 1989). Personal communication. For further discussion see: Gardner, H. (1990). The difficulties of school: Probable causes, possible cures. *Daedalus,* Spring; Walters, J., and Gardner, H. (1986). The crystallizing experience: Discovering an intellectual gift. In R. Sternberg and J. Davidson (Eds.), *Conceptions of Giftedness.* New York: Cambridge University Press.
3. U. S. Department of Education. (1990). *National goals for education.* Washington, D. C.: U. S. Department of Education, p. 14.
4. *American Educator,* Winter 1990.

Endnotes

5. A single exception are the few "key" schools that exist in large cities in China, special schools for demonstration and educational innovation. Even in a city as large as Beijing, however, there are very few "key" schools.

8. The Profession of Teaching

1. Lortie, D. C. (1975). *Schoolteacher: A sociological study.* Chicago: University of Chicago Press.
2. Ibid., p. 72.
3. Leestma, R., August, R. L., George, B., and Peak, L. (1987). *Japanese education today.* Washington, D. C.: U. S. Department of Education.
4. Barro, S. (1986). *A comparison of teachers' salaries in Japan and the United States.* Washington, D. C.: National Center for Education Statistics, U. S. Department of Education.
5. Japanese Ministry of Education [Monbusho] (1983). *Basic facts and figures about the educational system in Japan.* Tokyo: National Institute of Educational Research.
6. *The New York Times,* November 10, 1990.
7. Kidder, T. (1989). *Among schoolchildren.* Boston: Houghton Mifflin.

9. The Practice of Teaching

1. Rohlen, T. P. (1983). *Japan's high schools.* Berkeley: University of California Press.
2. Leinhart, G. (1986). Expertise in math teaching. *Educational Leadership, 43* (7), 28–33; Leinhart, G., and Greeno, J. G. (1986). The cognitive skill of teaching. *Journal of Educational Psychology, 78* (2), 75–95.
3. Mason, J. M., Anderson, R. C., Omura, A., Uchida, N., and Imai, M. (1989). Learning to read in Japan. *Journal of Curriculum Studies,* Vol. 21, No. 5, 389–407.
4. Davis, R. B., Maher, C. A., and Noddings, N. (1990). Constructivist views on the teaching and learning of mathematics. *Journal for Research in Mathematics Education,* Monograph Number 4. Reston, VA: National Council of Teachers of Mathematics.

10. Defining the Solution

1. U. S. Department of Education (1990). *National goals for education.* Washington, D. C.: U. S. Department of Education.
2. Article 158. Constitutional Provisions on Education and Culture of the Constitution of the Republic of China. Chapter 13, Section 5.
3. *Ann Arbor Daily News,* quoting study by American Federation of Teachers, April 7, 1991.
4. *Forbes,* May 14, 1990, quoting statistics from U. S. Department of Education, UNESCO, and OECD.
5. Ibid.
6. Bennett, William J. (1986). *First lessons: A report on elementary education in America.* Washington, D. C.: U. S. Department of Education.
7. Akers, John F. (1991). Let's get to work on education. *The Wall Street Journal,* March 20, A24.

For Further Reading

The reader who wishes further details about the research reported in this book is directed to the following selected publications.

I. Reading

Stevenson, H. W., Stigler, J. W., Lucker, G. W., and Lee, S. Y. (1982). Reading disabilities: The case of Chinese, Japanese, and English. *Child Development, 53,* 1164–1182.

Stevenson, H. W. (1984). Orthography and reading disabilities. *Journal of Learning Disabilities, 17,* 296–301.

Stevenson, H. W., Lee, S. Y., Stigler, J. W., Kitamura, S., Kimura, S., and Kato, T. (1986). Learning to read Japanese. In H. W. Stevenson, H. Azuma, and K. Hakuta (Eds.), *Child development and education in Japan.* New York: Freeman.

Stevenson, H. W., Lucker, G. W., Lee, S. Y., Stigler, J. W., Kitamura, S., and Hsu, C. C. (1987). Poor readers in three cultures. In C. Super and S. Harkness (Eds.), *The role of culture in developmental disorder,* Vol. 1 (pp. 153–177). New York: Academic Press.

Lee, S. Y., Stigler, J. W., and Stevenson, H. W. (1985). Beginning reading in Chinese and English. In A. Siegel and B. Foorman (Eds.), *Learning to read: Cognitive universals and cultural constraints.* Hillsdale, NJ: Erlbaum.

For Further Reading

II. Mathematics

Stigler, J. W., Lee, S. Y., Lucker, G. W., and Stevenson, H. W. (1982). Curriculum and achievement in mathematics: A study of elementary school children in Japan, Taiwan, and the United States. *Journal of Educational Psychology, 74,* 315–322.

Stevenson, H. W., Lee, S. Y., and Stigler, J. W. (1986). Mathematics achievement of Chinese, Japanese, and American children. *Science, 231,* 693–699.

Stigler, J. W., Lee, S., and Stevenson, H. W. (1990). *Mathematical knowledge of Japanese, Chinese, and American elementary school children.* Reston, VA: National Council of Teachers of Mathematics.

Stevenson, H. W., Lee, S., Chen, C., Lummis, M., Stigler, J., Fan, L., and Ge, F. (1990). Mathematics achievement of children in China and the United States. *Child Development, 61,* 1053–1066.

Stevenson, H. W. and Bartsch, K. (1991). An analysis of Japanese and American textbooks in mathematics. In R. Leetsma and H. Walberg (Eds.), *Japanese educational productivity.* Ann Arbor, MI: Center for Japanese Studies.

Fuson, K. C., Stigler, J. W., and Bartsch, K. (1988). Grade placement of addition and subtraction topics in Mainland China, Japan, the Soviet Union, Taiwan, and the United States. *Journal for Research in Mathematics Education,* Vol. 19, No. 5, 449–456.

Stigler, J. W. and Baranes, R. (1988). Culture and mathematics learning. In E. Rothkopf (Ed.), *Review of Research in Education,* Vol. XV. Washington, D. C.: American Educational Research Association.

III. Intelligence

Stevenson, H. W., Stigler, J. W., Lee, S. Y., Lucker, G. W., Kitamura, S., and Hsu, C. C. (1985). Cognitive performance and academic achievement of Japanese, Chinese, and American children. *Child Development, 56,* 718–734.

Stevenson, H. W. and Azuma, H. (1983). IQ in Japan and the United States: Methodological problems in Lynn's analysis. *Nature, 306,* 291–292.

IV. Socialization, Beliefs, and Expectations

Lee, S. Y., Ichikawa, F., and Stevenson, H. W. (1987). Beliefs and achievement in mathematics and reading: A cross-national study of Chinese, Japanese, and American children and their mothers. In D. Kleiber and M. Maehr (Eds.), *Advances in motivation*, Vol. 7, Greenwich, CT: JAI Press.

Chen, C. and Stevenson, H.W. (1989). Homework: A cross-cultural examination. *Child Development, 60,* 551–561.

Stevenson, H. W., Lee, S., Chen, C., Stigler, J. W., Hsu, C. C., and Kitamura, S. (1990). Contexts of achievement: A study of American, Chinese, and Japanese children. *Monographs of the Society for Research in Child Development, 221:55,* 1–2.

Stevenson, H. W. (1991). The development of prosocial behavior among Chinese and Japanese children. In R. A. Hinde and J. Groebel (Eds.), *Prosocial behavior, cooperation, and trust.* New York: Cambridge University Press.

Stevenson, H. W., Chen, C., and Lee, S. Y. (1991). Chinese families. In J. L. Roopnarine and B. Carter (Eds.), *Parent-child relations in diverse cultures.* Norwood, NJ: Ablex.

Uttal, D. H., Lummis, M., and Stevenson, H. W. (1988). Low and high mathematics achievement in Japanese, Chinese, and American elementary school children. *Developmental Psychology, 24,* 335–342.

Stevenson, H. W. (1990). Adapting to school: Children in Beijing and Chicago. *Annual Report.* Stanford, CA: Center for Advanced Study in Behavioral Sciences.

Stigler, J. W., Smith, S., and Mao, L. W. (1985). The self-perception of competence by Chinese children. *Child Development, 56,* 1259–1270.

Lummis, M. and Stevenson, H. W. (1990). Gender differences in beliefs and achievement: A cross-cultural study. *Developmental Psychology, 26,* 254–263.

V. Teaching and Learning

Stevenson, H. W., Stigler, J. W., Lucker, G. W., Lee, S. Y., Hsu, C. C., and Kitamura, S. (1987). Classroom behavior and achievement of Japanese, Chinese, and American children. In R. Glaser (Ed.), *Advances in instructional psychology*. Hillsdale, NJ: Erlbaum.

Stigler, J. W., Lee, S. Y., and Stevenson, H. W. (1987) Mathematics classrooms in Japan, Taiwan, and the United States. *Child Development, 58*, 1272–1285.

Stevenson, H. W. (1991). Japanese elementary school education. *Journal of Elementary Education, 92*, 109–120.

Stigler, J. W. and Perry, M. (1988). Mathematics learning in Japanese, Chinese, and American classrooms. In G. Saxe and M. Gearhart (Eds.), *Children's mathematics*. San Francisco: Jossey-Bass.

Stigler, J. W. (1988). The use of verbal explanation in Japanese, Chinese, and American classrooms. *The Arithmetic Teacher*, Vol. 36, No. 2, October 27–29.

About the Authors

Harold W. Stevenson received his Ph.D. in psychology from Stanford University and has been president of the Society for Research in Child Development, the International Society for the Study of Behavioral Development, and the Division of Developmental Psychology of the American Psychological Association. He is a professor of psychology at the University of Michigan. A Fellow of the American Academy of Arts and Sciences, he has also been a Guggenheim Fellow and a Fellow at the Center for Advanced Study in the Behavioral Sciences, and is the recipient of the G. Stanley Hall award for research by the American Psychological Association. He and his wife, Nancy Stevenson, are the parents of four children.

James W. Stigler is currently professor of psychology at UCLA. He served on the faculty of the University of Chicago for eight years after receiving his Ph.D. in psychology from the University of Michigan. He has been the recipient of Carnegie-Mellon University's William G. Chase award for research by a young scientist in the area of cognitive psychology, the American Psychological Association's Boyd McCandless Young Scientist award, and a Guggenheim Fellowship, and has been a Fellow at the Center for Advanced Study in the Behavioral Sciences. He and his wife, Karen Aptakin Stigler, are the parents of two sons.